Quilting

A Step by Step Guide

Margery Cutbush

HAMLYN
London · New York · Sydney · Toronto

My warmest thanks to my colleague Mrs. M. A. Parker, for her help and interest. To the N.F.W.I. for the loan of several pieces of work from their loan collection. To Fay Morgan Laws for the use of her quilt and designs which she so generously allowed me to use. To Constance Howard and her students at the Goldsmiths College whose work is illustrated in the book. The Dougal nursery wall hanging is by kind permission of BBC Merchandising.

Thank you to my husband for his perceptive assistance and help.

Published by
The Hamlyn Publishing Group Ltd
London · New York · Sydney · Toronto
Astronaut House, Feltham, Middlesex, England
© Copyright the Hamlyn Publishing Group Limited 1974

ISBN 0 600 38117 X

Printed in England by Chapel River Press Andover, Hampshire.

Contents

Introduction

In this simple guide to quilting it is possible for any needlewoman with or without the talent for designing to make some of the quilted articles which are described in this book. They need only the absolute minimum of sewing experience and the ability to use the sewing machine.

This step by step guide to creative quilting explains in great detail the different quilting techniques and shows how they can be used or adapted on comparatively simple pieces of work. When the various techniques have been attempted they can be used in a variety of practical or decorative ways, on many different materials carried out in fine hand stitchery or with a sewing machine.

A beginner will gain confidence by following the instructions and simple diagrams, and as the techniques are mastered will build up a knowledge and understanding of this craft. An experienced needlewoman will be able to use the ideas and adapt them to produce original and more elaborate work.

Design is an essential part of quilting and consequently it is a perfect means of self expression. However, the beginner should not worry unduly about this aspect; as skill and experience are acquired you will be encouraged to create your own designs. Be content in the beginning to copy or modify until the basic skills have been perfected. Concentrate on the method of working and understand the necessity for planned and careful finishing so essential to good work.

The art of quilting

Quilting is an ancient craft and unfortunately very little is known about its history or origin. The word quilt is derived from the Latin 'culcita', and the dictionary defines the word quilt as 'a bedcover of two cloths sewed together with something soft between them'.

Quilting has been mentioned in many old documents and household inventories dating back to mediaeval times and the earliest recorded use of the word was in 1290. The oldest known and best example of quilting is the famous Sicilian quilt dated circa 1400, part of which can be seen in the Victoria and Albert Museum. Made in the linen quilting technique it is purely decorative, the surface being covered with scenes worked with dramatic artistry and masterly precision, it illustrates the early life of the Knight Tristan.

The quilting process has been known and practised widely from early times in most European and Eastern countries, as well as in the Moham-medan regions of Africa.

In mediaeval times its use was adapted for body armour and Knights or foot soldiers wore quilted jackets or gambesons. The quilted jackets were worn under armour and chain mail, to prevent the metal chafing the skin, or as a useful substitute for body armour. The workmanship of these garments was probably quite simple since the thickness of the padding and the coarse linen would make fine stitchery impossible. This came later when women adapted the quilting process to suit their own personal requirements.

In the Tudor period quilting began to appear on clothing and quilted night caps became fashionable. By the seventeenth and eighteenth centuries quilted doublets, breeches, waistcoats, dresses and petticoats were being made of silk and quilted with beautiful floral designs and intricate patterns. In the reigns of Queen Anne and the first two Georges this skill reached a peak of perfection and the work was enriched by the addition of silk embroidery.

Linen quilting using the stuffing method was also worked on garments such as petticoats, stomachers, pockets and on household furnishings. Bed quilts were made with matching bed curtains and cushions. The popularity of this work was probably due to the fact that it was practical and decorative. The pieces were easy to launder and being made entirely of linen materials would last indefinitely.

By the close of the eighteenth century, with the introduction of new fabrics and different fashions, quilted clothing went out of fashion. Quilts and coverlets continued to be an important item in most house-holds, being made by professional or itinerant quilters, or by the house-wife herself. In the nineteenth century the rapidly expanding textile factories were producing machine made quilts of various kinds. Of these, one known as a marcella quilt was woven so ingeniously that it copied the raised effect of the quilting process. Eventually these quilts became cheaper and more plentiful and though they were not as warm as the hand made ones, they became fashionable.

It was only the need to exercise economy which helped to keep the craft alive. In the mining districts of County Durham and South Wales, shortage of work and unemployment made it imperative for women to be thrifty and earn money in the best way they knew – by making quilts. In consequence the art of this ancient craft has come down to the present day with an almost unbroken tradition.

There was a time during the last war and in the years that followed when the need for austerity had a very restricting influence on our lives and on the things that were produced. When this period of restriction ended there was a swing in the opposite direction which resulted in gayer and more colourful clothes, and exciting new designs for men and women. At the same time new developments were taking place which resulted in new materials being used for furniture and soft furnishings. These new materials have influenced the new trends in furniture design and in consequence the modern home has become a perfect background for quilted murals and decorative panels, and the bold use of colour.

Basic equipment

There are some items of equipment which are basic to all the techniques described in this book and most of them are simple tools used by most needlewomen.

Some quilting can be done in the hand, and not mounted on a frame, but only when the layers of material and padding have been tacked closely and accurately together so that the work will not pucker.

Work Box
A work box, needlework basket or work bag is needed, for it is an essential container for all the basic items of equipment. It can be handmade or a more decorative antique box.

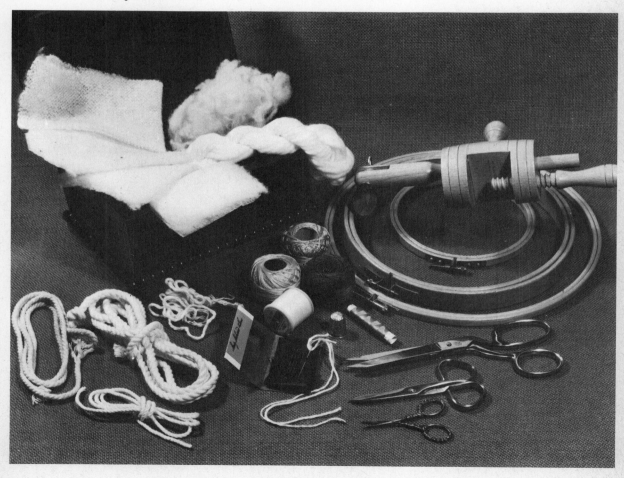

Needles

These should be made with smooth well shaped eyes. Badly made needles with poorly finished eyes will cause the thread to wear and fray, thus spoiling the appearance of the stitchery. All needles should be chosen to suit the type of thread which is being used. A needle case is the best place in which to keep needles to ensure that they are not mislaid.

Types of needle

betweens : No.7–No.10 are small fine needles suitable for English quilting.

chenille : No.25 should be used for linen quilting. It has a longer eye which will take most of the thicker threads used in this work.

tapestry : a large size for stuffing.

sharps : for tacking, making up and any fine sewing.

Steel Pins

These should be fine and of good quality, sharp and new, so that they will not mark the fabrics when they are used.

Scissors

These should be sharp and of good quality to ensure a clean-cut edge to the fabric. 1 pair of large scissors for cutting fabrics. 1 pair of small scissors for snipping the threads and trimming away the surplus fabric in the making-up process.

Threads

This word describes all cotton, mercerised, button hole silk, pure silk, embroidery threads and filaments used for the stitchery. Each should be carefully chosen for its suitability in respect of the material on which it will be used. It should always be thick enough to cover any transfer lines.

Thimble

A metal thimble is less bulky than a plastic one and more comfortable. It is important to get used to wearing a thimble because, as well as protecting the middle finger, it assists the stitchery. Make sure that the thimble fits the finger snugly but not tightly. Old thimbles can be bought sometimes and these are usually finely made and elegant to wear.

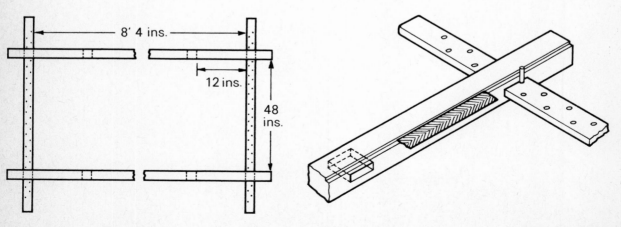

Fig 1

Frames

It is often thought that to use a frame is awkward and difficult. However it is important to realise that work mounted on a frame makes even stitchery much easier to achieve and it will ensure that the materials do not pucker. The use of the frame allows greater comfort in working, freeing both the hands to do the stitchery, one on the upper side and the other on the underside of the work. There are two distinct types of frames:

Hoop or Tambour A round frame which can be used for small pieces of work. The sizes of these frames range from four to ten inches in diameter. They consist of two rings of wood, plastic or metal which fit one over the other. A small screw on the outer ring enables the ring to be adjusted over the thickness of the fabric, which is stretched across the inner ring.

Tambour frames can be bought attached to a wooden clamp so that the frame can be fixed to a table, and some are made mounted on a simple stand which can be stood on a table while in use. Floor hoops or floor frames are particularly useful as they can be adjusted to the correct working height and angle.

Slate Frame A slate frame is used for large pieces of work and consists of two rollers of wood for the top and bottom of the frame and two flat pieces of wood for the sides. These side pieces have holes at frequent intervals along their length and pass through the slots at each end of the rollers. The position of the rollers is adjusted on the side pieces to suit the length required and they are retained in position by pegs inserted in the appropriate holes. Both rollers have along their edges pieces of wide tape or webbing which is used for mounting the material on the frame.

Slate frames can be bought mounted on stands. They can be tilted to any angle for comfortable working and leave both hands free.

Quilting Frame An old quilting frame was generally large enough to accommodate a full-sized quilt. The frames were made of hardwood and consisted of two long bars and two cross bars or stretchers. The stretchers fitted through slots in the long bars and were held in place with pegs which were put in holes drilled along the length of the stretchers. When the quilt was set up for use, it was placed on the backs of chairs so that several women could work round the edge of the frame. These old frames can sometimes still be obtained. (Fig. 1)

Tape Measure or Yardstick

These are useful items necessary for measuring fabrics and the size of quilt tops, etc.

Sketchbook

A sketchbook is invaluable for in it can be recorded not only ideas, but notes, paper shapes, photographs and any other information which would otherwise be forgotten. It will be a record for future reference of far more use than notes and sketches made on old envelopes and scraps of paper.

Lighting

Quilting is one of the most relaxing forms of needlework, and in consequence it is important to work in the best possible conditions. Always sit in a comfortable chair and work in a good light, which should come over your left shoulder if you are right handed. In poor lighting conditions use a reading lamp with a flexible arm which can be adjusted so that the light shines on the work. This is an excellent facility provided it is suitably angled to eliminate glare.

Fabrics
Choosing the correct fabric is an important factor in all methods of quilting. Certain materials are more suitable than others but only those of good quality should be used. The fabric should be closely woven, soft and have a smooth surface.

Quilting can be used on many different kinds of material depending on the use to which it will be put, and its suitability for the technique of quilting which has been chosen.

Natural Fabrics
Cotton – Cambric, poplin, sateen, viyella, velveteen
Wool – Flannel, fine wool, nuns veiling
Silk – Pure silk, tussore and shantung, spun silk, velvet, crêpe de chine, slipper satin
Linen – Fine even weave
Synthetic or man made fibres
Leather
A transparent material is not suitable unless the padding is intended to be seen as in shadow quilting. Choose fabrics which have a slightly lustrous surface but are not shiny as this will detract from the design. Fabrics should be washable and wear well. It is also important that they are colourfast.

Fillings
Quilting may be padded with many different types of material.

Cotton wadding or batting has been in use for many years, and can be bought by the yard. It has a size backing which makes it easy to handle. One layer is generally enough but two layers could be put together to make a thicker padding.

Cotton wool sold in packets should be carefully unwrapped and opened out ready for use. This should not be confused with medicated cotton wool sold by chemists which has been made to absorb moisture.

Cotton wadding and cotton wool have serious drawbacks. They do not wash well and tend to become lumpy unless the surface is quilted closely. Neither do they puff-up well.

Old blankets can be used and are an economical way of making a bed quilt. The blanket should be preshrunk by washing it in very hot water before use.

Domette is an interlining of wool sold by the yard, ideally suited for quilted garments, since it is light and warm.

Synthetic wadding or batt made of dacron or terylene is light, fluffy and durable. It can be obtained in a variety of thicknesses and weights and its chief good qualities are that it can be washed extremely easily and is resilient.

Flannel or cotton blankets or flannel sheets can be used after being preshrunk. They make a soft strong filler which is easy to handle, but the surface of the work will be very flat.

Wool, the traditional padding can be an economical and practical filler, but it is not easily obtained. It is light and warm as well as being easy to wash.

Linings
On quilts which are reversible the same material is often used for the top and bottom covers. A different colour may be chosen either in a paler or darker tone. The underside of a quilt should always be carefully considered and a fabric chosen which bears some relation to the top surface.

Where the underside of the work is hidden as in a cushion cover, an inexpensive cotton or closely woven lawn can be used.

All lining fabrics should be firm, colourfast and of good quality. Poorly made fabrics will tend to shrink and may not be colourfast. Choose a good material which is closely woven and durable, which will keep its shape and enhance the finished piece of work.

Quilting techniques

Quilting is one of the oldest forms of needlework and it has been practised widely in many countries in the world. It is not surprising therefore to find that different styles and techniques have developed and that these vary considerably.

English Quilting or Wadded Quilting

Where warmth has been required for bed clothing or garments it was discovered long ago that this could be best achieved by sewing two fabrics together with a layer of soft padding in between. From the beginning this stitchery became an important part of the quilting technique. (Fig. 2)

Materials
Fabric –   for the top and bottom covers
          Pure cotton fabrics, dull satin, sateen, pure silk, tussore, shantung or spun silk.
Padding – Lambs wool, cotton wool, or wadding, domette, synthetic wadding, dacron batting or a blanket.
Thread – Use cotton No. 40 matching the surface material, or pure silk on silk fabric.
Needles – Between size No. 8, not more than $1\frac{1}{8}$ inches long.
Frame –   A frame is an absolute necessity – an embroidery frame can be used for articles of moderate size.

Small articles such as tea cosies, slippers, glass cases and small bags could be quilted in the hand if all the layers of material are basted or tacked firmly together. It is preferable to use a tambour or hoop frame.

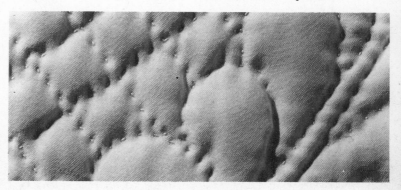

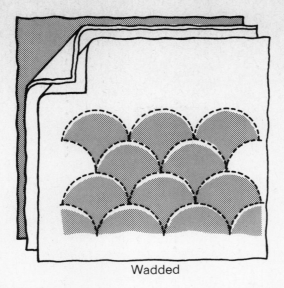

Wadded

Fig 2

Templates In wadded quilting the designs are made up with decorative shapes called templates. These templates are cut from firm card. When planning a design for wadded quilting, select templates which bear some relation to each other. Considerable thought should be given to the scale of the motifs and their proportion, which must be suited to the size of the article which is to be planned. Too large or too small shapes will spoil a beautifully made piece of work and the whole effect will be marred if the scale of the design is incorrect.

Planning a design This is not difficult or too skilled for a beginner because most of the shapes are bold simple units which stand out against the all-over background patterns. It is important to make sure that the design will look well on the completed article. Select or make a group of templates and arrange them on a sheet of paper. Try several arrangements until a satisfactory design has been achieved. Draw the full design on a sheet of paper for reference.

NOTE: Do not fill the whole space with pattern but allow for balance and contrast between the curving shapes of the design and the straight background stitchery. Contrast can be made between the lines of stitchery which are close together, giving low relief, and those which are at a medium distance apart, giving medium relief, and those which are spaced still further apart giving the effect of high relief. However it must be remembered that it is the stitchery which holds the inner padding in place so that the shapes must be arranged so that there are no unquilted areas measuring more than 2 inches across.

Needle Marking In wadded quilting, the design is usually worked with running stitches which pass through the three layers of material so that the work is reversible. Consequently the design has to be transferred on to the top fabric so that it will not show. This is done by marking round the templates with a needle and is called needle marking. The template is placed in its correct position on the fabric of the top cover and its shape is outlined on the fabric with a needle held at an angle. If pressed firmly the needle will leave an impression of the template clearly defined on the fabric.

Marking the design If the article to be quilted is small, the design can be marked on the top cover when all the materials are mounted in the frame.

Cushions, cot quilts, or full sized quilts can be needle marked before being set up on the frame.

NOTE: It is important to find the exact centre of the fabric of the top cover by measuring or folding and to mark this with chalk or cotton. Other important points such as the position of the corners, the width of the borders, and diagonal lines from the centre to the corners can also be marked.

The fabric is then placed right side up on a table over a thick cloth and the design is firmly needle marked by drawing the needle round the template. Work carefully and accurately to ensure that the finished work will be satisfactory. Only the main shapes of the whole design need be marked. Details in the pattern can be marked by hand as the work proceeds.

Dressing the Frame for Wadded Quilting

Set up the frame and stitch the fabrics of the top and bottom covers to the tape at the top edge of the frame.

Stitch the bottom cover to the tape at the bottom edge of the frame. Place the layer of padding smoothly over the bottom cover, and bring the top cover over and pin it securely down to the fabrics at the bottom of the frame. Lace the quilting materials to the stretchers of the frame with lengths of tape pinned to the edges of the work. The tension should be firm but not taut.

Finishing the Quilt

Wadded quilts which are reversible will look well if finished simply. A quilt design will have been carefully planned before it was mounted in the frame, and when it is completed it should then need no further decoration.

The edge of the quilt can be finished in several ways. The raw edges of the top and bottom covers can be turned in and stitched together with two rows of running stitches to match the stitchery of the quilt. The first line should be as near to the edge of the quilt as possible and the second line of running stitches $\frac{1}{4}$ inch further in. Make sure that the padding comes up to the very edge of the quilt and never finish the edges with machine stitchery. The two rows of stitchery should give the appearance of another two rows of quilting.

Piping is another finish which makes a neat, firm edge, and this can be used on a cot quilt. Turn in the edges and insert a piping cord which has been covered with a strip of the same material cut on the cross. The piping should be stitched on the edge of the underside of the work with the top cover slip stitched to the base of the piping on the front of the work.

Binding cut on the cross from the main fabric can be used to finish a quilt. Before being stitched in place it should be stretched slightly to ensure that it lies flat.

Small quilted articles such as cushions and tea cosies are improved when finished at the edge with a piping cord. The size of the cord should be carefully considered. This should not be too thick or it will appear clumsy and out of proportion to the scale of the work. It should always be covered with a strip of crossway cut fabric. Both the join in the piping cord and the crossway strip should be carefully planned so that they are smooth and neatly made.

NOTE: Care should be taken to ensure that the stitchery is neatly worked and if possible invisible. All pieces of work should be finished firmly and the ends of threads secured so that the article will be durable.

As I have already said, the edges of the work should never be finished by machine stitching.

Linen Quilting

Linen quilting is one of the most beautiful forms of traditional needle-work and it has been practised widely for many centuries. Unlike wadded quilting which it in no way resembles, it did not evolve as an art form from the need for warmth and comfort. Linen quilting is entirely decorative. Most of the early quilts were made of white or cream coloured linen and there were pieces which had fine coloured embroidery as further decoration.

Some pieces of work were completely padded between the layers of linen with stuffing threaded through the back of the work. Sometimes the stuffing was omitted from parts of the work and gradually the technique was modified and adapted to achieve different effects.

The craft as practised today has been adapted and simplified to suit modern requirements.

Linen quilting is comprised of three distinct techniques which are described as follows:

1. *Padded Quilting* This consists of two thicknesses of linen being backstitched together with a padding of soft piping cord being afterwards inserted between the layers under the design.

2. *Corded Quilting* This consists of a cord being held on the underside of the linen and back stitched to it so that the design stands out in relief. Corded quilting is usually worked combined with another linen quilting technique.

3. *Flat Quilting* This consists of two thicknesses of material being back stitched together forming a background of low relief. No padding is used in this form of quilting.

Designs
The designs for linen quilting are dictated by these three techniques. A design can be based on two of these, so that part of the design is padded and stands out in high relief and part is worked in a flat quilting background, which tends to recede.

Padded Quilting Designs for padded quilting should be bold in outline and made up of small rounded or oval shapes which can be easily stuffed.

Corded Quilting Designs for corded quilting can be made up of parallel lines the thickness of the cord apart. The design should be bold and flowing and without complicated detail.

Embroidery worked in fine chain stitch can be beautifully combined with this technique.

Flat Quilting These designs usually form a repetitive background of simple stitchery, worked in rows, forming diamonds, squares or shell design. The size chosen should be in proportion to the rest of the design as these background stitches are used as a foil for the more elaborate parts of the design.

When designing for linen quilting (Fig. 3) the embroidress should try to achieve a balance between those parts of the design which stand out in relief and those which tend to recede. Harmony and balance in the use of rounded shapes and straight lines is equally important. A good design should consist of bold simple shapes and finicky detail should be avoided. The design is always transferred to the surface of the linen for this work.

Fig 3

Materials

Linens – Linen quilting is worked on finely woven linen for the front
of the work and a loosely woven linen scrim is used on the back.

Threads – Quilting D.M.C. Cotton Perle No. 12 or No. 8 or a medium
button hole twist.
– Coloured embroidery Clarkes Stranded Thread.

Piping Cord – A soft cotton piping such as No. 1 is used for corded
designs and a thick one is satisfactory for stuffing.

Needles – Chenille No. 25 for the stitchery. A blunt wool needle for
the padding.

Scissors – A small pair of sharp scissors.

Frame – It is essential to use a frame. A small tambour or hoop frame
with screw adjustment for small articles and a rectangular embroidery
frame for larger pieces of work.

NOTE: Before any work is attempted it is important that the linen scrim,
and all piping cord should be well shrunk. Place the loosely folded
materials and the cords for piping and stuffing in a vessel. Cover with hot
water. Bring to the boil and leave for a few minutes. Hang the fabrics and
cord up to drip dry without wringing. Iron the linen and scrim carefully
when almost dry to remove any wrinkles.

Transfer the design on to the surface of the fine linen so that any
straight lines are square with the warp and weft threads.

Dressing the Frame for Linen Quilting

First mark the centre of the tape with a pencil, on the top and bottom
rollers. The centre of the scrim backing should be pinned to this mark
and the fabric sewn firmly with close oversewing stitches from the
centre outwards, on both rollers.

A piece of fine string should be sewn in a fold along both sides of the
backing to make a firm edge. A length of string is used to lace the fabric
to the stretchers so that the backing is held taut, the ends of string being
firmly attached at both ends of the frame.

The piece of linen, design side up, is placed centrally on the backing
and first pinned squarely in place so that it is quite flat. The linen should
be sewn neatly along the edges to the scrim backing.

It is important that linen and scrim should be as taut as possible.

Stitchery

This is generally worked in back stitch and with the linen mounted in a
frame. Start with work without a knot, running the end of the thread
through the two layers of linen, under the design. The back stitches
should be small, firm and perfectly even. They should be worked like a
stab stitch with the needle going in and out of the fabric vertically. To
achieve even stitchery it is important to be relaxed, and also to sit at the
work for as long as possible so that the quilting becomes rythmical and the
stitches evenly made. Fasten off by making a few tiny over-sewing
stitches on the wrong side of the work on the already completed stitchery.

Quilting Process of Linen Quilting

Padded Quilting. When the stitchery has been completed, the bold shapes
of the design are stuffed with piping cord. To do this, unravel a length of
cord and thread several strands into a blunt wool needle. Pad the design
from the wrong side of the work by threading the cord through the scrim
and repeat the process until enough cord has been left between the layer

of linen and scrim to raise the design in relief. Cut off the ends of the cord close to the design and tuck the frayed ends under the scrim with the eyelet end of the needle so that the back of the work is neat with no ends showing.

The padded shapes should be full but not overstuffed. Examine the work by holding it to the light and regulate the padding where necessary into difficult corners with the needle, so that every part of the design is filled evenly.

NOTE: Always pad the design with the work mounted in the frame.

Corded Quilting. In this quilting process a length of piping cord is held under the surface of the linen beneath the parallel lines of the design, with the left hand. The cord is stitched to the underside of the design with back stitches worked first on one side and then on the other side of the design. The stitches hold the cord in place and form a closed herringbone stitch over the cord on the underside of the work. The cord should not be stretched or this will flatten it. The cord should be firmly stitched so that it will stand out in relief on the linen surface. Never cross the cord at any intersections in the design. Cut the cord neatly and close to the work and start again. Where the design is very rounded it will be necessary to take an extra back stitch at intervals along the outer edge of the corded design so that the stitchery can be kept level on both sides of the outline.

Flat Quilting. This is worked on two thicknesses of linen and stitched in backstitch and no padding is inserted between the layers.

Finishing
The making up and finishing should be carefully done by hand. The edges of the work should be finished where necessary with a narrow piping cord in a crossway strip.

If the work has become soiled it can be washed while it is still in the frame. Care should be taken to see that the frame does not get wet. Remove the quilting from the frame when it is quite dry.

Italian Quilting *(Illustrated in colour, Page 17)*

This form of quilting is purely ornamental and is used mainly on cushions and bed quilts. Its appeal is from a decorative point of view entirely, since the work is not completely padded and in consequence has very little warmth. This form of quilting is quite different from other forms and its method is widely known and understood.

In its simplest form it is the sewing together of two fabrics – the surface material and the muslin backing, with decorative stitchery in a raised design. This raised effect is achieved with a design consisting of parallel lines about $\frac{1}{4}$ inch apart, through which a length of soft quilting wool is pulled, when the stitchery has been completed.

Materials
Surface fabric – Silk, fine wool, velvet, spun silk
Backing   – Closely woven muslin
Thread   – Matching silk
Stuffing   – Quilting wool, strands of yarn or knitting wool.

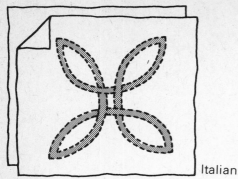

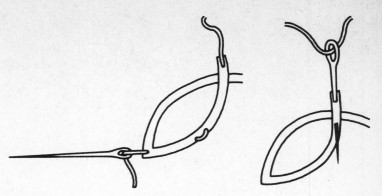

Italian

Fig 4

Method (Fig. 4)

The design is traced on the backing material and this is tacked or basted, wrong sides facing, to the surface material. The outline of the design, which consists of parallel lines, is stitched with neat, even running stitches until completed.

Using a blunt wool needle threaded with strands of quilting wool or several strands of acrylic yarn, run the needle through the backing along the channel of the design. Come up through the backing as far away as the needle will allow, or at a convenient point in the design. The yarn can be cut off or the needle can be reinserted in the same hole and threaded along the design. Leave a small loop of yarn where the needle comes out and is reinserted in the design. Care should be taken to ensure that the yarn is not pulled tightly along the design. It should be loose and smooth so that the design is perfectly raised without puckering on the right side of the work.

Shadow Quilting (*Illustrated in colour, Page 21*)

Shadow quilting is worked through two thicknesses of fabric, the upper surface being semi transparent, so that the coloured wool with which the design is padded will show through.

The work will have a delicate appearance and the finished effect is elegant. This process is ideally suited to garments made of fine material such as blouses, evening gowns and bed jackets. The latter would need an interlining of domett for warmth.

Materials

Surface fabric – Crêpe de chine, pure silk
Backing – Closely woven muslin
Padding – Skeins of brightly-coloured colourfast embroidery wool
Thread – Pure silk

Check that the material is translucent enough to allow the wool to show delicately through the fabric. There are two methods of working:

Method 1 The design is drawn on the backing, which is then tacked or basted on the wrong side of the surface fabric, so that there is no possibility of either slipping.

The design is outlined in small running stitches in a matching thread until all the lines have been covered. Remove the tacking threads and turn

(OPPOSITE PAGE) *Panel of fine, close machine quilting, the surface sprayed to simulate hand printing. (Bernard Schofield)*

the work on the wrong side. Strands of coloured wool are threaded through the back of the design with a blunt wool needle and the ends trimmed where they enter and come out of the muslin. Do not allow the needle to penetrate the silk. Hold the work up to the light and regulate the padding where necessary so that every part of the design is filled with padding.

Method 2 The design is transferred on to the surface fabric marking it with a very fine outline. The backing is sewn with rows of tacking to the wrong side of the surface material so that the two fabrics are kept firmly in place. If the piece of work is large it should be mounted on a frame, as the stitchery is carried out in back stitches which cover the transfer lines. This is not easy to work neatly in the hand.

When the design has been completely stitched the tacking threads are removed and the work should be turned on the wrong side for stuffing. This can be done while the work is still on the frame and the wool is inserted into the back of the design as described in Method 1.

Fig 5

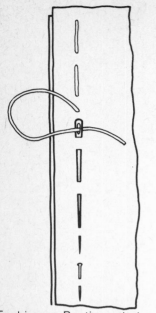

Tacking or Basting stitch.
Fig 6

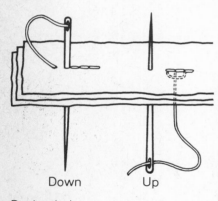

Down   Up

Back stitch
Fig 7

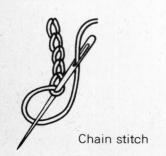

Chain stitch

Notes on Stitches

The stitchery is an important part of the work. In wadded quilting the stitchery should be worked in running stitches so evenly spaced that it should be impossible to tell on which side the finished quilt has been worked. It is important to mount the quilting in a frame to free both hands for making the stitches. The needle should go through the three thicknesses in every stitch and the stitches must be of even length with the same spaces between them on both sides of the quilt. It will take practise before the stitches are small and evenly worked, so first concentrate on making the stitches evenly spaced. Skill will come from practise so that it will eventually be possible to work eight or ten stitches to an inch. It is always advisable to work for as long as possible at a time and to try and establish a rhythm which will produce straight lines and smooth curves.

Back Stitch
This stitch is simple to work and should be regular in direction so that the lines are straight and the curves rounded and smooth.

Method of working The correct way to work is from right to left, bringing the needle through on the stitch line and going backwards making a small stitch through the fabric with the needle held vertically. Bring the needle through again in the same way a little ahead of the first stitch, make another stitch inserting the needle at the point where it first came through. The back stitches should be small and evenly made.

Back stitching is usually worked on quilting where the back of the work will not be seen. The needle should never enter the work at an angle but should always be pressed through the fabrics vertically. The stitching should always be worked with the materials tautly mounted in a frame. This will enable the back stitches to be evenly made. Sit as long as possible to achieve a good stabbing rhythm which will result in fine, relaxed, perfectly made stitchery.

Chain Stitch
Chain stitch is a very good stitch to use for bold outlines worked in a thick thread. Chain stitch can be used for the coloured embroidery which is frequently combined with linen quilting. This is worked with a single thread of stranded cotton in rows of fine close stitchery and built up into floral motifs of great distinction.
Method of working Bring the thread out at the top of the stitch line and hold it down with the left thumb. Insert the needle where it last came through the fabric and bring the needle out a short distance away on the line of working. Pull the thread through, keeping the working thread under the needle point.

Buttonhole Stitch
This is worked in the same way as blanket stitch except that the stitches are close together. It can be used for attaching motifs to the top cover of a quilt. Where designs are to be applied which have an irregular outline, the method of attaching the shapes can be simplified by working buttonhole stitch to cover the raw edges.
Method of working Bring the thread out on the lower stitch line, insert the needle immediately above in position on the upper line, and take a straight downward stitch with the thread under the needle point. Pull the stitch flat so that it forms a loop and repeat.

Running Stitch

This should be regular in direction when worked in straight lines or outlining curved shapes. The stitches on both sides of the work should be of equal length with equal spaces between.

Method of working Push the needle through the work with the thimble-covered middle finger so that it enters at an angle, guiding it towards the thumb, which is extended in front to press the material flat ahead of where the needle will come up as each stitch is made. The left hand is under the work to guide the needle when it pierces the back, and the fore and middle fingers anticipate the position of the needle and help it back to the face of the quilt by pushing up the underside.

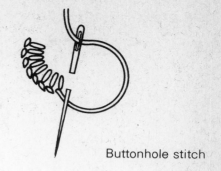

Buttonhole stitch

Transferring a Design on to Material

An embroideress who has adapted a design or created an original one has always to transfer this design on to the fabric. In this book designs are given for the beginner to follow or adapt (Fig. 10) and the first step will be to trace one of these on to tracing paper before it can be transferred on to the fabric for quilting.

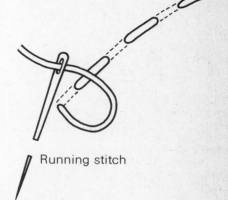

Running stitch

Fig 8

Tracing Method

Do not use typing carbon paper but a special coloured dressmakers' carbon which will not smudge. First the fabric should be pinned flat and squarely placed on a board with drawing pins. Pin the tracing above this in the correct position and then slip a sheet of coloured carbon paper with

Fig 10

the carbon face down, under the tracing. Use a sharp pencil and outline the design firmly and carefully so that a good impression is left on the fabric. If necessary this line can be made more distinct with watercolour paint applied rather dry, with a very fine tipped brush. Leave to dry.

Transfer Method

Place the transfer paper over the design and outline the design carefully using a very fine pen nib and a commercial transfer ink. Leave to dry.

A substitute transfer ink can be made with a teaspoon of commercial washing blue mixed with three or four teaspoonfuls of fine sugar. The liquid should be mixed in a small container until the sugar is dissolved.

This ink will offset a design several times. Painted on the reverse side of the transfer it will give a reverse of the design if this is not symmetrical.

Transfer Pencils

These are very quick to use as well as being accurate. The design is traced off on to paper, placed face down on the fabric and ironed off.

Pouncing

This is one of the oldest methods and a very useful one when a design will be used many times. It is however, not easy and it takes time and care to master the technique. Take the traced design and place this on a pad of soft material. Use a needle and prick holes all round the outline of the design, evenly spaced about one-sixteenth of an inch apart. With a piece of fine emery paper remove the rough edge of the holes on the underside of the tracing. Pin the material to be quilted on a drawing board with the pricked design in the correct position above it, or the reverse side of the design if required. Gently dab the pouncing powder through the holes with a little felt pad.* Check to see that the right amount of powder has been used by carefully lifting one corner of the design. Remove the pricked design with care so that the pounced design is not disturbed. Paint over the dotted lines of the design with a fine brush and water colour paint, using very little water, joining the dots with a finely made line. Allow to dry thoroughly and shake well to remove all traces of the powder.
* *On light fabrics use powdered charcoal, on dark, powdered french chalk.*

Templates

These are shapes cut out of cardboard, the outlines of which can be scratched with a needle directly on to the fabric to be worked.

Tacking Method

A simple design can be transferred on to the fabric by first making a tracing of the design on fine transparent paper. This should then be basted in position on the fabric and the design outlined with small running stitches in a contrasting thread. The transfer is then carefully cut and pulled away from the basted outline which can be removed as the quilting progresses. This is usually the best method of offsetting a design on a coarsely woven material but it is also suitable for quilting where only the bold outline is needed and the rest of the design can be worked freely.

Muslin Transfers

These are used for Italian quilting and are made by pinning the muslin squarely and firmly over the design so that the material will not move. The design shows through and is outlined carefully with a biro pencil on the muslin. The transfer will be on the underside of the work and the outlined design will not be seen when the quilting is completed.

Things to make

A Spectacle Case

A small article for a beginner to make is a decorative case for reading glasses. Although a design has been given, an original one could be attempted, and then made up following the instructions described in the text. Only small pieces of fabric are required but the material chosen for the outside should be finely woven and smooth, so that the surface stitches can be evenly worked. A piece of soft fabric such as velvet, velveteen or fine wool should be used for the lining and preferably the colour should match or tone with the surface fabric.

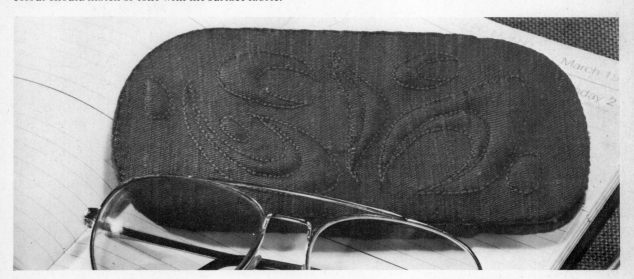

Materials
A piece of silk or linen measuring 10 in. square
A piece of closely woven muslin the same size
A piece of velvet approximately 9 in. square
2 pieces of canvas or thick vylene cut to the shape of the case
2 pieces of cardboard from a cereal carton, cut to the same shape
D.M.C. cotton perle, No. 8 or similar thread for the quilting
1 – No. 25 Chenille needle
Matching sewing thread for making up
Soft wool
1 – sewing needle
Fabric adhesive

Method
The design should first be traced on to a piece of tracing paper. Tack the

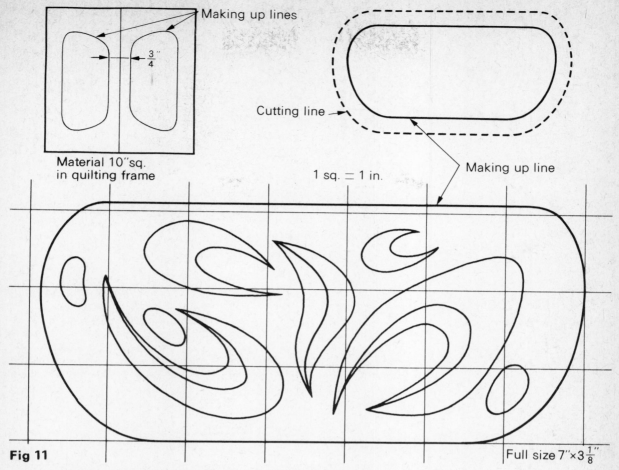

Making up lines

Material 10"sq.
in quilting frame

Cutting line

Making up line

1 sq. = 1 in.

$\frac{3}{4}$"

Fig 11

Full size 7"×3$\frac{1}{8}$"

outline of the case twice on to the surface fabric as shown in the diagram, using a brightly coloured thread. Pin this material on to a board or hold the edges firmly in position using cellotape, making sure that the material is squarely placed. Put the traced design above the material so that it is in the correct position inside the top outlined shape. Place a piece of dressmakers carbon paper face down on to the fabric under the tracing. Trace off the design, using a sharp pencil. Turn up the edges of tracing and carbon to see that the outline of the design is clear and is not too thick.

Remove the tracing and repeat this process on the second shape. The traced material should be taken from the board and the piece of muslin tacked to the underside so that both fabrics are perfectly flat. Mount in an embroidery frame so that the material is taut and square. Commence the stitchery using a stabbing back stitch, sewing the two fabrics together along the outline of the design. The stitches should be small and even and regular in direction so that the traced outline is completely covered. Complete the stitchery for both sides of the case.

Quilting process
Pad the designs as described for linen quilting (page 15), using soft wool. When both shapes are complete the work can be removed from the frame.

Making-up
Trim round the two outlines leaving a small seam allowance of $\frac{1}{2}$ inch.

Place the thin cardboard shapes in position on the wrong side of the work, using a little fabric adhesive. The edges of the fabric are turned over the cardboard shape and held in position with adhesive.

Work on the long sides first and cut small notches in the fabric round the curved edges so that the material can be stuck neatly and smoothly to the shape of the case. Repeat on the second side.

Cut the velvet lining in half and lightly glue a canvas shape in the middle of each half and trim the velvet $\frac{1}{2}$ inch larger all round the canvas. Repeat the process of shaping and glueing the velvet over the canvas.

There are now two velvet shapes for the outside of the case and two velvet-covered shapes for the lining. These four are then assembled in pairs – one quilting and one lining piece with their wrong sides facing, stitched together invisibly. These two sides are stitched firmly, velvet face to velvet face, leaving an open end for insertion of glasses.

The stitchery of the outside seam can be concealed by covering the edge of the case with braid, narrow velvet ribbon, or a bias strip cut from the same material as the glasses case.

A Tea Cosy (*Illustrated, Page 34*)

In this piece of work the technique to be explored is wadded quilting, in which three layers of material are secured with running stitches.

A beginner can copy or adapt the shapes which are illustrated and have been used for the example, or an original piece of work could be attempted.

The example has been made for a small tea pot but the arch could be increased. A paper shape should be cut and placed round the pot to ensure that it is wide enough, sufficiently high, and allows for the thickness of the tea cosy pad. When a shape has been made it can be used as a pattern.

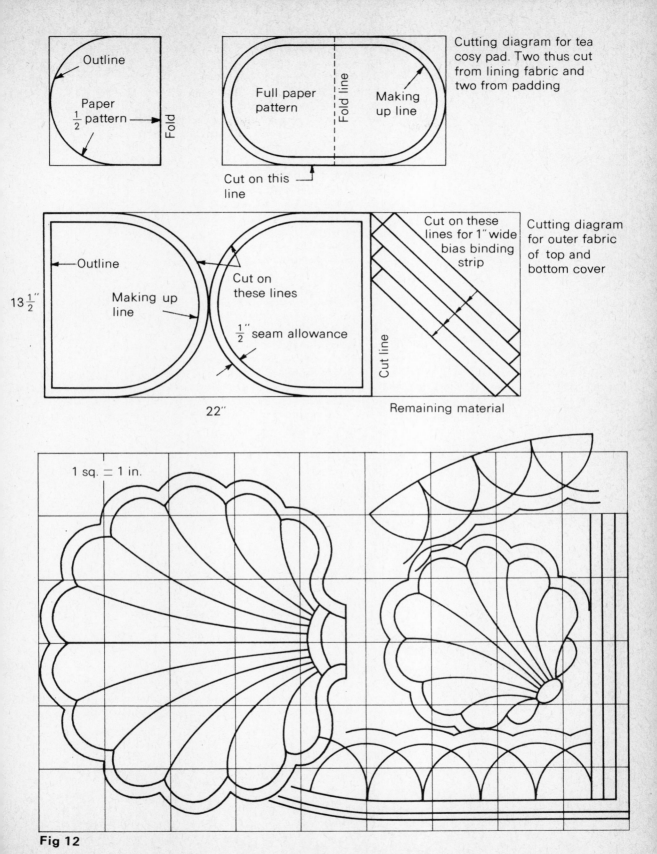

Outline

Paper $\frac{1}{2}$ pattern

Fold

Full paper pattern

Fold line

Making up line

Cutting diagram for tea cosy pad. Two thus cut from lining fabric and two from padding

Cut on this line

Outline

Making up line

Cut on these lines

$\frac{1}{2}''$ seam allowance

$13\frac{1}{2}''$

22''

Cut on these lines for 1" wide bias binding strip

Cut line

Remaining material

Cutting diagram for outer fabric of top and bottom cover

1 sq. = 1 in.

Fig 12

35

Planning the design The tea cosy shape should be drawn on paper so that the templates can be grouped within the overall space. When the area is small, the templates should be in proportion to the finished article but the shapes must be bold enough to stand out in relief against the stitched background. A good design should consist of three parts – a main pattern, one or more subsidiary patterns, and the background. A shape can be emphasised by outlining it with another row of stitches.

In the tea cosy design the templates should be grouped so that space is allowed for a small border and some background stitchery.

Materials
27 in. of silk or fine poplin
12 in. of cotton wadding or synthetic batting
1 spool of silk thread to match the silk
1 between needle
A length of fine piping cord
A small slate frame

Method
Divide the fabric as shown in the cutting diagram. Outline the shape of the tea cosy pattern twice on the top cover, using brightly coloured cotton. This is the making up line. Make another row $\frac{1}{2}$ inch outside this line to mark the cutting line (Fig. 12, centre and bottom).

Mount the fabric of the bottom cover in the frame and spread the padding evenly on top. Put the top cover in place and pin it squarely over the surface of the two other layers. Baste it in position so that all three thicknesses are smooth and flat. Hold the three layers along the stretchers of the frame with tape strappings to ensure even tension over the surface of the work.

Quilting process
Mark the design on the surface of the fabric by outlining the shapes of the templates with a needle so that an impression is left on the material.

Details on the templates such as the veins, or dividing lines, or a second line to outline a shape can be marked in as required or judged by eye and stitched without marking. The background design can be filled in later.

Commence the stitchery with thread which has a knot at the end. This thread can be pulled gently through the layers so that it lies under the surface along the line of working. The quilting is worked throughout in running stitches and these should be evenly made so that the work will be reversible. Consequently the stitches must penetrate the three layers and to perfect this technique it is necessary to work with the left hand on the underside of the frame, so that the fore-fingers can feel the needle each time it comes through the quilting. Make two or three running stitches at a time where possible.

Finish off the sewing thread by taking a stitch back through the layers along the line of stitchery coming up and down over one or two stitches. Run the needle through the padding, coming up some distance away and clip off the thread close to the work.

Background lines can be marked in with a ruler and needle when the main design has been stitched. Take care the lines are parallel.

The back of the tea cosy can be worked with a repeat of the design used on the front or it can be modified. Any unsatisfactory detail can be put right on the second piece of work so that it is a good idea to mark only one side of the work at a time.

Making-up

Remove the quilting from the frame and trim each piece of work along the cutting line. Trim the padding on both sides, back to the making-up line.

1st side. Trim and slip stitch the two outer layers of fabric together along the making-up line of the bottom edge. Finish the top edge of the cosy with a narrow piping, fitted into the length of crossway binding. At the lower ends the cord should be neatly concealed and finished off in line with the bottom edge. The piping is attached with neat back stitches to the front of the quilting along the making-up line, and the fabric of the underside is slip stitched so that it conceals the raw edges and stitching of the piping cord.

2nd side. Trim and turn in the two outer layers of fabric and slip stitch them neatly together along the making-up line. The two pieces of work are placed together and pinned in position. The front of the tea cosy is slip stitched to the back invisibly along the piping line so that the two sides are held firmly together.

Tea Cosy Pad

The tea cosy pad should be made of a good quality fabric such as sateen and should be washable to be really practical. Choose a colour which will tone with or match the tea cosy cover, and a filling of synthetic wadding.

The pad must be a perfect fit and should be cut from the pattern of the tea cosy.

Method

Cut the pattern of the tea cosy as shown in figure 12 (bottom) by placing it on a sheet of folded brown paper. From this pattern cut two pieces of sateen, and two pieces of synthetic wadding. Place these on a flat surface in the following order.

1. Layer of wadding
2. 2 pieces of sateen, right sides facing
3. Layer of wadding

Pin the layers carefully together and baste them firmly along the outside edges. Leave an opening as shown in the diagram. Machine or back stitch along the line of basting. Remove the basting cotton and turn the cosy pad inside out through the opening. Push the bottom half of the pad up into the top half with the raw edges of the opening at the top. Turn in and pin the edges of the opening neatly and slip stitch together invisibly. Secure the thicknesses of material together with a few neat stitches so that the inside of the cosy is attached to the outside. Fit the completed pad inside the quilted tea cosy.

Silk Cushion   (*Illustrated in colour*, Page 20)

Very simple tradition shapes have been arranged to make a design suitable for a cushion. The quilting has been worked in back stitches on slipper satin. The process of working and making up is described, step by step, and in this quilting technique the design is first planned on paper and then transferred on to the surface of the fabric by tracing.

1 sq. = 1 in.

Cutting line $8\frac{1}{4}''$ radius

Fig 13

Materials

27 in. of slipper satin 36 in. wide
3 spools of buttonhole twist to match
1 spool of pure silk to match
2 pieces of synthetic wadding 18 in. square
2 pieces of cotton lawn 18 in. square
1 chenille needle No.25
1 sewing needle
$1\frac{1}{2}$ yds of narrow piping cord
1 slate frame

Method

Cut the satin as shown in the cutting diagram, having first pressed the fabric with a warm iron to remove any creases.

Planning the design Pin a sheet of drawing paper on a board and with a pair of compasses describe a circle $5\frac{3}{8}$ inch radius, making only a feint line. Place the compass point on the line and using the same radius set out eight divisions round the circumference of the circle. Reset the compass and describe two larger circles, one $7\frac{3}{4}$ inch radius and one 8 inch radius. The first of these two circles is the making up or seam line and the larger is the cutting line.

Trace the feather and rose template from the diagram and cut out their shapes in card.

Place the feather template on one of the marks on the inner circle and draw round its outline. Repeat in the seven remaining sections. There should be a small space between each feather. Draw a continuous free-hand line round the ring of feathers on the inner and outer edge $\frac{1}{4}$ inch away from the feather shapes. Draw the outline of the rose motif in the exact centre of the circle. Mark in the background lines so that they are parallel, square and $1\frac{1}{2}$ inches apart.

Transferring the design

Trace the completed design on to tracing paper and transfer it to the fabric of the cushion top using dressmakers' coloured carbon paper, also marking the outlines of the cutting and making up lines. Transfer in the same way the rose design as well as the cutting and making up lines to the fabric of the cushion back, using the same tracing.

Quilting process

Dress the slate frame by mounting one of the pieces of lawn centrally on the rollers. Place the wadding and then the cushion, top design side up, in the centre and pin squarely in position. Baste firmly along the edge so that the three layers are held together.

The stitchery is worked in back stitches along the lines of the design. The stitches should be small even and regular in direction and entirely cover the transfer lines. Work until the design is completely stitched. Outline the making-up line with basting stitches worked in a coloured thread.

Repeat the process using the appropriate piece for the back of the cushion.

Making-up

Trim the two pieces of work along the cutting line. Join the crossway strips to make a binding long enough to encircle the cushion. Baste the piping cord firmly in place along its length and stitch the covered cord round the outer edge of the cushion, using the coloured thread as a guide. Trim and join the crossway strip neatly and join the ends of the piping cord so that there is no bulge. Place both sides together and slip stitch the second side in place along the base of the piping cord.

A place should be left open for the insertion of a soft cushion pad and a fine zip fastener can be inserted which will enable the cover to be removed for cleaning. Alternatively the opening can be closed neatly with slip stitches.

Evening Handbag *(Illustrated in colour, Page 25)*

An evening bag is an interesting article to make for personal use or for a gift. It could be made from scraps of material left over from an evening dress or skirt.

Materials
$\frac{1}{2}$ yard of heavy quality satin or silk
$\frac{1}{2}$ yard of lining to match
2 spools of button hole twist to match
2 pieces of wadding 9 in. square
1 piece of lawn 20 in. by 12 in.
1 spool of sewing silk for making up
1 crewel needle No.7
1 fine sewing needle
2 yards of fine piping cord
1 gilt bag frame $5\frac{1}{4}$ in. between the mounting holes
1 slate frame

Method
Cut the satin as shown in the cutting diagrams so that there are –
  2 pieces of fabric 9 in. square
  2 cross-way strips measuring 27 in. long by 1 in. wide.
  1 gusset 19 in. long by 2 in. wide
Trace the complete design of the bag on to a piece of tracing paper, including the cutting and piping lines. Transfer this design on to the right side of both squares of satin, making sure that the design is central and squarely placed.

Mount the lawn in a slate frame so that it is taut and flat. Place the padding on the lawn with the two pieces of satin in position on top. Baste through all three layers of material so that the satin is held square and flat.

The quilting is worked in back stitch using button hole twist. Make small neat stitches of even size.

Making-up
When all the stitchery has been completed the work can be removed from the frame. The satin should be trimmed to the cutting line and the muslin and padding to the piping line, on both back and front of the bag.

Outline the piping line on both pieces with small running stitches using contrasting cotton.

Cut the piping cord in half. Baste the piping cord into the crossway strips. Baste the covered cord in position on the back and front of the bag, using the coloured stitching line as a guide. Back stitch in position firmly and remove basting cottons.

Pin the gusset in position between both sides of the bag and sew it in place invisibly, using small slip stitches.

Position the completed bag on the bag frame, holding it in place with several small tie tacks through the holes on both sides of the frame. Stitch the bag to the frame, hiding the stitches in the seam of the piping. Small back stitches and double sewing threads will make a firm, strong fitting.

Cut and make a lining to fit the finished bag and attach with small neat stitches.

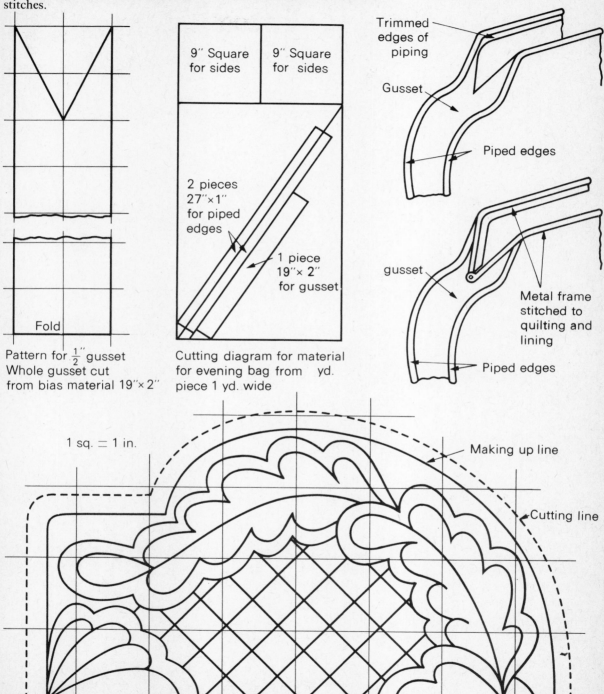

Pattern for $\frac{1}{2}''$ gusset
Whole gusset cut
from bias material 19"× 2"

9" Square for sides

9" Square for sides

2 pieces 27"× 1" for piped edges

1 piece 19"× 2" for gusset

Cutting diagram for material for evening bag from   yd. piece 1 yd. wide

Trimmed edges of piping

Gusset

Piped edges

gusset

Metal frame stitched to quilting and lining

Piped edges

1 sq. = 1 in.

Making up line

Cutting line

Fig 14

Fig 15

Quilted Tray (*Illustrated in colour, Page 28*)

This is a perfect way to mount a piece of linen quilting. The design is interesting, with a border of corded quilting, some padded shapes and a background of flat quilting. This design would look equally attractive worked on a small cushion.

The material which was chosen for this piece of work is a fine half-bleach linen, and the stitchery is worked in a light gold thread.

Materials

1 piece of fine linen 18 in. by 12 in.
1 piece of fine linen scrim 18 in. by 12 in.
1 ball of D.M.C. Cotton Perl No.8
1 chenille needle No.25 for the quilting
1 blunt wool needle for the padding
7 yards of No. 1 piping cord for the corded quilting
4 yards of No.3 piping cord for the padded quilting
1 slate frame

NOTE: The linen, scrim, and piping cords should be thoroughly shrunk. The linens should be hung up to drip dry and, when almost dry, ironed carefully to remove any wrinkles.

Method

The full design should be traced on to tracing paper and transferred carefully on to the surface of the linen so that the lines of the design are straight and square.

The linen scrim should be mounted as taut as possible in the frame and the linen stitched to it so that the design is flat and square.

The stitchery is all worked in back stitching and the stitches should be firmly made and as evenly worked as possible.

The corded quilting should be firmly stitched so that the fine cord held under the work is raised in relief on the surface. The cord should be carefully cut at every intersection. The straight lines are stitched and padded later.

All the stitchery should be carefully worked so that it is regular in direction on the straight lines and curved shapes.

When all the stitchery and corded quilting has been completed the padded parts of the design are filled with unravelled piping cord, threaded between the layers with a blunt wool needle. This should be done while the work is still on the frame.

If the work has become soiled it can be washed on the frame. No water should be allowed to touch the frame.

When the linen is dry it should be removed from the frame and mounted on a thick piece of cardboard $\frac{1}{2}$ inch wider and longer than the design.

The finished piece of work should be professionally framed to ensure that the frame is sealed correctly.

Making Quilted Garments

Quilting is ideal for many garments because it is both practical and decorative. It is important, however, that any garments which are to be quilted should be fashionable and well cut. A stylish garment of basically simple design will look very beautiful, if the quilting is carried out with simplicity and restraint.

Some practice is desirable so experiment, using your own design, and make a pocket, a belt or a tie. Quilt a shoulder yoke, cuffs or the hemline of a dress before deciding on a more ambitious piece of work.

Choosing the top fabric
Fabrics for quilted garments should be carefully chosen. Ideally they should be closely woven with a smooth surface. There is a large variety to choose from which will all look attractive when quilted but some should be avoided. Those with a shiny surface such as cheap satin and taffeta, which split easily and are too stiff, are unsuitable. Fabrics such as pure silk, linen, pure cotton, slipper satin and sateen are obvious choices. Viyella or similar materials of wool and cotton mixture are excellent, and velvet will look particularly attractive.

Interlining
Carded lamb or sheep's wool is an ideal choice but a double layer of domette will be easier to buy and more straightforward to use. Synthetic wadding of Terylene or Dacron is best for washable garments, but it is important that the top fabric should be closely woven so that the fibre ends of this underlay will not work through the weave.

A Frame – to use or not to use
Quilting can be worked in the hand and many beautiful pieces of work have been made without the use of a frame. Great care should be taken to ensure that the materials do not pucker and to prevent this the layers of fabric should be stitched firmly, in both directions, to keep them flat and smooth before any quilting can be attempted. The layers of fabric should be spread out flat on a large table and tacked together from the centre outwards.

Garments to be quilted should be carefully planned when the pattern is laid out on the fabrics. Allowance should be made for the fact that the quilting will take up some of the fabric and reduce it in size in both directions. Place the pattern pieces farther away from each other so that an extra wide seam allowance can be left. All the quilting should be completed before the fabric is cut out, fitted and made up.

Stitching
This is usually carried out with small running stitches or by machine. Quilting worked by hand should be stitched with a fine thread such as sewing silk or fine cotton. This can match the fabric, depending on the desired effect. Machine quilting with a thicker thread such as button hole twist could be used to produce a bolder line.

Quilted Trouser Coat (*Illustrated in colour, Page 29*)
Quilting can be put to many practical uses by adding warmth to garments such as bedjackets and trouser coats.

A simple trouser coat can be made from a basic pattern. By working in the wadded quilting technique the garment could be made completely reversible. In the model described here the two fronts only have been quilted and a simple flat belt buttoned to the waistline at the back. Velvet has been chosen for the surface fabric in a shade of bright orange with a copper-coloured lining of pure silk for contrast. Domette has been used as an underlay and the stitchery has been worked in an orange-toned silk thread. This shows up the design very clearly on the coat lining, adding an extra touch of luxury and elegance to the garment.

Materials
(*To make a trouser coat, size 36 in. bust.*)
1¾ yards of velveteen 36 in. wide
matching silk thread
1¾ yards of silk lining
matching silk thread
30 in. of domette 54 in. wide
1 slate frame

Method
Figure 17 shows a cutting diagram which is identical for the velvet and the silk. The pieces for the coat front should be left uncut and the velvet mounted in a slate frame face down. Place the domette on the velvet and the piece of silk in position on the domette. Baste the three thicknesses of fabric together so that they lie flat and square. Pin the pattern of the front on the fabrics and mark its outline making-up line twice on the fabric as shown on the cutting diagram.

The design for the coat has been given scaled down and will have to be enlarged. Make card templates on the individual shapes and use them to needlemark the design on to the silk, being careful to ensure that the design is straight and square and that the two fronts are symmetrical.

Work the design in neat evenly made running stitches, going through the three layers of material, and work until both sides are completed. Remove the quilting from the frame and cut out the fronts, on the cutting line. Trim back the domette underlay to all the making-up lines.

Making-up
Work only on the velvet; join the centre seam on the back of the coat, stitch the darts, the shoulders and underarm seams.

Work only on the lining: join the centre back seam and the shoulder seams and press these open. Turn the coat inside out and slip stitch the darts and underarm seams so that they lie flat.

Turn down the velvet round the armhole edge on the making-up line and slip stitch the lining neatly along the outer edge.

The velvet of the lower edge of the coat should be turned up and secured with stitches which will not show on the right side. The neck and front edges of the coat should be turned back and the velvet held down with some loosely made stitches taken through the domette. Pin the lining up to the edge of the velvet at the neck, front and bottom edge of the trouser coat and slip stitch the two fabrics together smoothly and invisibly.

Quilted Evening Skirt (*Illustrated in colour, Page 49*)
This very simple evening skirt is easy to make using a basic skirt pattern. It can be made in a simple wraparound style and shaped with folds at the waist, being fastened at the waistband where the skirt overlaps with a

Design for Trouser coat

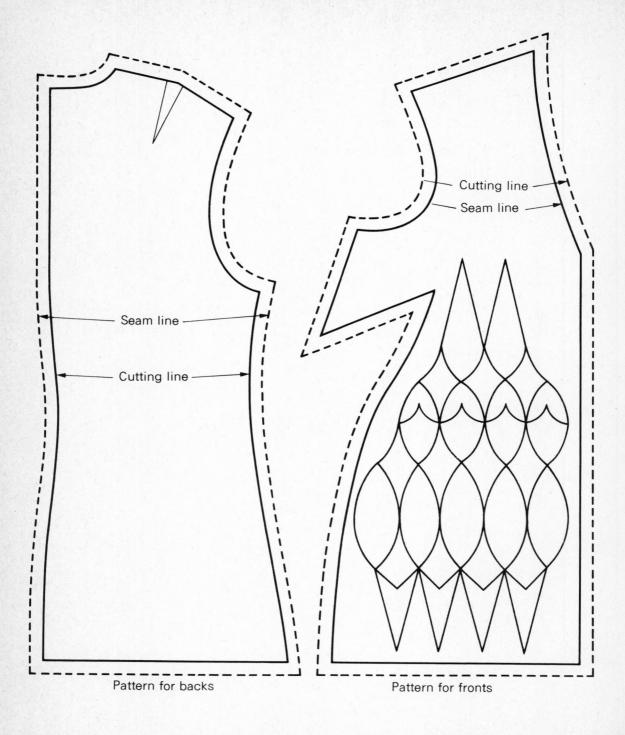

Cutting line

Seam line

Seam line

Cutting line

Pattern for backs

Pattern for fronts

Fig 17

46

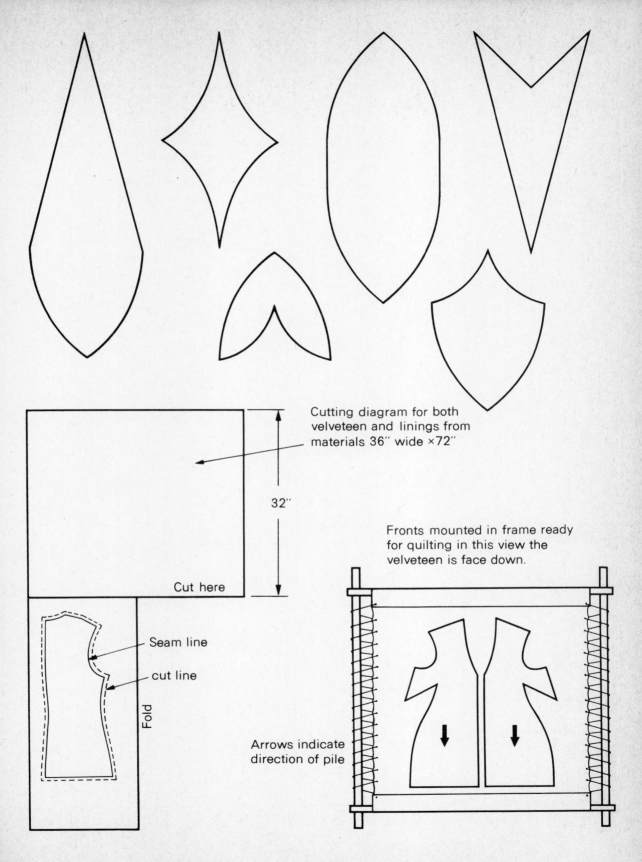

Cutting diagram for both
velveteen and linings from
materials 36″ wide ×72″

32″

Cut here

Seam line

cut line

Fold

Fronts mounted in frame ready
for quilting in this view the
velveteen is face down.

Arrows indicate
direction of pile

strip of Velcro. An experienced needlewoman would have no difficulty in making a skirt like the model described, which has been simply shaped with gathers into a waistband.

The fabric which has been chosen for this evening skirt is rather finely woven and light-weight so that it is not very suitable for cold weather. It is printed with a very colourful design which is particularly appropriate to the quilting process, which adds weight to the fabric and makes it hang well. It produces a garment of beauty and elegance which can be worn on many occasions with great distinction.

Many beautiful fabrics are to be found which can be handled in exactly the same way, being quilted by an ordinary sewing machine or by hand quilting sections of the design to give it greater detail and emphasis.

Materials
$1\frac{3}{4}$ yards of fabric 54 in. wide
matching sewing thread
$1\frac{3}{4}$ yards of thin synthetic wadding 54 in. wide
$1\frac{3}{4}$ yards of lining 54 in. wide
1 zip fastener 7 in. long
1 yard of $1\frac{1}{2}$ in. wide stiffening for skirt band

Method
First cut and mark the fabric which is to be quilted, allowing $2\frac{1}{2}$ inches to 3 inches for a hem, $\frac{1}{2}$ inch seam allowance at the top edge and centre back seam, and a 3 inch strip of fabric for a $1\frac{1}{2}$ inch wide waistband. Overcast any raw edges which may fray. Lay the fabric face down on a flat surface with the padding and lining in position on the top. Pin the materials together at regular intervals to ensure that they lie flat. Cut off the surplus wadding and lining. Baste the three thicknesses together across the fabric with long stitches in lines approximately 6 inches apart.

Quilting process
The design can be quilted by hand or with a sewing machine, following

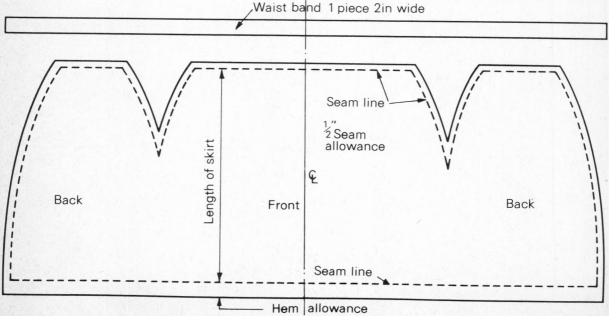

Fig 18

48

the bolder, simpler outline and not the small intricate detail. It is preferable not to take the quilting stitchery up to the waistline. This will simplify the making-up process.

Making-up
When the quilting process has been completed, the basting cottons should be removed. If a sewing machine has been used, the quilting threads should be pulled through the back of the work where they can be tied securely and trimmed off.

The skirt should be fitted and made up as carefully as possible. The surface fabric should be gathered at the top edge and basted in position under the skirt band, with the lining and interlining laid in folds behind it so that the bulkiness is diminished. The skirt band stiffener should be inserted and a zip fastener fitted in the centre back opening. The lower edge of the skirt should be turned up to form a hem and stitched invisibly, and any raw edges should be neatened with overcast stitches.

Quilted Waistcoat (*Illustrated in colour, Page 20*)
Quilting can be used as a decoration or for the more practical purpose of making a garment which is warm to wear. In this case it serves both purposes.

A waistcoat or jerkin can be made so that it is reversible, by using the wadded quilting technique, making the garment of two different fabrics in two different colours. The design should first be drawn to scale, ensuring that it looks well. Templates can then be made of different shapes of the design and these would be used to outline the design on the fabrics. A more simple but not reversible waistcoat could be made which is just as fashionable, using surface quilting only.

First a design should be drawn which fits suitably into the shape of the waistcoat front pattern. This should follow any interesting shape based on modern or traditional motifs. The pattern which has been chosen for the model is based on Victorian braidwork from a smoking jacket. The waistcoat fronts are made of velvet and are faced with a matching corded silk. The same corded silk has been used for the waistcoat back and the finished garment lined with a toning heavy quality satin.

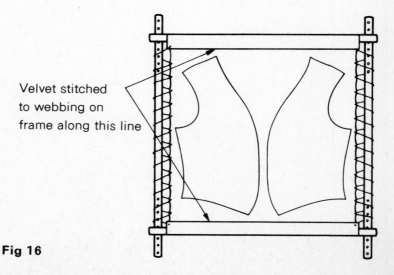

Velvet stitched to webbing on frame along this line

Fig 16

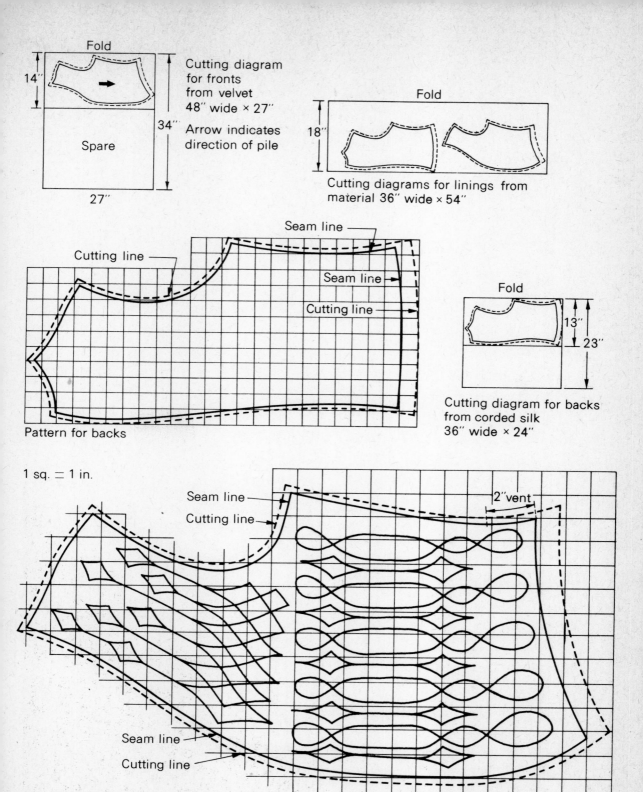

Fold

14"

Spare

27"

34"

Cutting diagram
for fronts
from velvet
48" wide × 27"

Arrow indicates
direction of pile

Fold

18"

Cutting diagrams for linings from
material 36" wide × 54"

Seam line

Cutting line

Seam line

Cutting line

Pattern for backs

Fold

13"

23"

Cutting diagram for backs
from corded silk
36" wide × 24"

1 sq. = 1 in.

Seam line

Cutting line

2" vent

Seam line

Cutting line

Design for quilted waistcoat Pattern for fronts

Fig 19

51

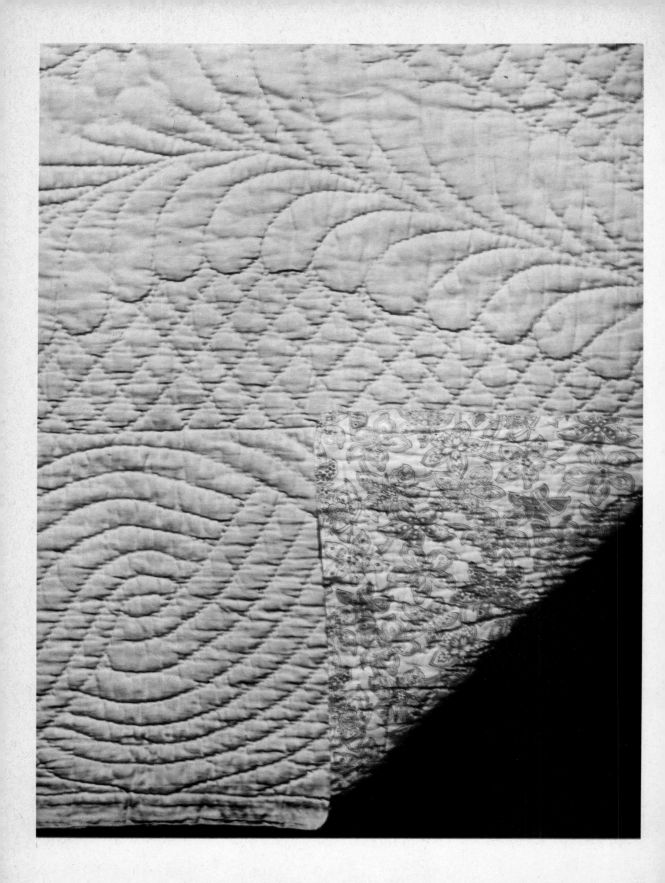

Man's Waistcoat
(*Size: 38 ins.*)

Materials
$\frac{3}{4}$ yard of cotton furnishing velvet
$\frac{3}{4}$ yard of domette
1 spool of silk thread to match
$\frac{3}{4}$ yard of corded silk to match velvet
$1\frac{1}{2}$ yards of lining fabric to tone with velvet
$\frac{3}{4}$ yard of muslin
6 buttons $\frac{1}{2}$ in. diameter
matching sewing thread for finishing
1 slate frame

Method
The pattern shapes should be enlarged from figure 19 on to dress-maker's squared paper. In the diagram, each square represents one inch, and $\frac{1}{4}$ inch seam allowances have been made all round except that a 1 inch seam allowance is made along the lower front edge. If the quilting design shown is to be used it should also be enlarged to fit inside the waistcoat front shape.

The outline, seam line, and design should be drawn on to the muslin and a reverse copy made of the second front alongside the first.

The velvet should be set up in the frame so that it is face down, covered by a layer of domette with the muslin transfer on top.

NOTE: It is important that the muslin transfer should be placed so that the velvet pile runs down the body of the waistcoat.

The three layers of fabric should be flat and smooth and be basted together firmly. The outline or cutting line and the seam lines should be marked with basting stitches through the three layers of material.

Quilting process
The complete outline of the design on both fronts should be neatly stitched with evenly-spaced running stitches going through the three layers of fabric. Then the quilting can be removed from the frame.

Making-up
Cut out the two fronts along the basted cutting line.

Cut out the front and back waistcoat pattern pieces in lining fabric, and machine the back pieces of fabric together down the centre back seam and press open.

Cut out the back pattern in corded silk and cut two 26 inch lengths of bias binding 1 inch wide from the remainder of the silk. Join the centre back seam and press open.

Fold the bias binding in half and stitch in place down the right front, so that a $\frac{1}{4}$ inch binding forms a flat facing from the shoulder seam to the point at the bottom front edge. Stitch the bias binding in place on the left front to correspond, but leaving 6 equally spaced vertical openings 3 inch long for button holes as shown in the diagram. The edges of the facing should be neatly turned in along the spaces, and stitched together with tiny firm stitches, and the velvet stitched down to the backing so that the buttonholes are clearly defined.

Baste the two quilted fronts to the corded back and fit the garment for size and make any necessary adjustments. Remove basting threads. Turn up the 1 inch allowance at the lower edge of the two fronts and stitch to the backing.

Pin the front lining pieces in position on the fronts so that the lining covers the stitching line of the front facing and at the lower edge shows $\frac{3}{4}$ inch of velvet. Slip stitch firmly with neat small stitches, face the lining up to the turned in edge of the vent, and slip stitch flat. Turn in the edge of the velvet along the arm hole edges and slip stitch the lining neatly down to the velvet, just inside the arm hole edge.

Machine the two fabrics of the waistcoat back together along the lower edge seam and press flat.

Place this piece on a flat surface, right side up, with the corded silk towards the top. Put the two fronts in position with the velvet face down on the corded silk, and pin along the shoulder and underarm seams.

Bring the silk lining up and pin it over the fronts so that these are enclosed between the two layers of the back fabric, which should be wrong side outside. Baste the shoulder and underarm seams together through the lining and quilted fronts.

Baste the two lining fabrics firmly together along the arm hole seam, pushing the quilted fronts carefully away to ensure that the quilting is not caught by the basting stitches.

Machine the seams on both sides of the work, starting at the shoulder seam on the neck edge, stitching round the arm hole and down the under arm seam to the back edge of the vent. Remove the basting cottons.

Turn the waistcoat to the correct side by pushing the fronts in turn carefully through the unstitched opening of the neck seam.

The neck seam allowance on the corded silk should be turned in and the lining should be slip stitched to it just inside the edge. A line of small running stitches should be worked $\frac{1}{4}$ inch below.

The lining should be carefully pressed flat along the lower back seam, on the shoulder seams, and at the arm hole edge.

Mark the position of the buttons so that they correspond with the buttonholes and are in line $\frac{1}{2}$ inch from the silk facing. Use buttonhole thread and sew the six buttons firmly in place.

Useful Quilted Items

Quilted Tea Towel

Modern tea cloths are beautifully designed. These towels can be made into charming wall hangings, pictures or cushions.

Choose a colourful design which is not too detailed but is printed with a suitable subject matter for the room in which it will be placed, i.e. fruit, spices or vegetables for the kitchen, or a nursery scene or a character well known to children for a hanging in a child's bedroom. Many of these towels are made in several colours and one can usually be found which will fit into the general colour scheme of the room.

Dirty Clothes Tidy (*Illustrated in colour, Page 32*)

A useful clothes bag can be made for a children's room using a tea towel or a printed piece of furnishing material. The towel or fabric should have a vertical design as the bag is made to hang over a coathanger.

The bag can be hung behind a door or in a cupboard and dirty socks, hankies or underwear can be pushed into the bag and later taken from it for laundering by opening the zipper fitted in the bottom seam.

Materials
1 piece of printed fabric or a tea towel
1 piece of synthetic wadding
1 piece of muslin
1 piece of lining
1 coathanger – wooden
1 zip fastener
1 sewing needle
1 reel cotton thread
1 reel sewing thread

Method
Press and remove any creases from the fabric and place it face down on the surface of the table. Cover this with the wadding and place the muslin on top so that all three materials are smooth and flat. Pin together in several places and tack the three layers together in both directions, so that they are held firmly.

Quilt the fabrics using the cotton thread, choosing a colour which will match the outline of the design. The stitchery should be worked in small, even running stitches so that the design or parts of the design are raised in relief.

When the quilting has been completed the top edge of the work should be shaped to fit a wooden coat hanger. Cut two pieces of lining the same size as the bag.

Pin the two pieces of lining and the quilting, so that they lie in the following order:
Bottom: Quilting right side up
Middle: Lining wrong side up
Top: Lining wrong side up

Tack all three together, leaving the bottom open, and a space on the side seam for an opening. Machine along the tacking lines: remove tacking threads. Turn the work carefully inside out and press with an iron to remove any creases. At the lower edge stitch the inside lining with slip stitches to the turned in edge of the quilted material. Attach a zip fastener to this edge and the outer lining.

On the side opening, slip stitch the edge of the inner lining to the back of the quilting and make a neat seam on the edge of the outer lining.

Should the design be suitable, an opening can be made on the quilted front and its edges finished with bias binding to match the bag.

Finally a small eyelet hole should be worked in the middle of the top edge of the bag, through which the hook is screwed into the coat hanger.

Nursery Wall Hanging, Dougal (*Illustrated in colour, Page 25*)
Materials
1 Tea towel
a piece of cotton wadding, a piece of muslin and a piece of
   lining all the same size as the tea towel
2 lengths of dowel
4 plastic knobs or finials to fit the dowel ends
1 crewel needle
stranded embroidery cotton
tacking cotton
sewing thread to match tea towel

Method
Press the tea towel to remove any creases or fold marks. Place the towel face down on a flat surface with the wadding spread smoothly on top, and cover this with a piece of muslin. Pin all three materials together. Baste through the three layers with rows of stitches in both directions holding them together.

Quilting process
Stitch round the outline of the design using three threads of stranded cotton in the same colour as the printed outline of the design. Use chain stitch to produce a bold effect, making the stitches as even as possible.

When all the quilting has been stitched the basting threads should be removed. Turn the work on to the wrong side and trim the wadding so that the outer edge of the towel can be folded back and stitched down to make a neat firm edge. Press the lining and trim it to cover the back of the hanging with $\frac{1}{2}$ inch seam allowance. This is turned under all round leaving a place at the top and bottom for the insertion of the dowel rods. These can be held in position with a row of stitches. The edge of the lining is sewn down to the back of the towel with slip stitches.

The dowel rods are used to stiffen the top and bottom edges of the hanging and are finished off at each end with plastic knobs or finials. A piece of cord is attached to the ends of the top rail to serve as a hanger and complete the work.

Baby Basket (*Illustrated in colour, Page 28*)
A dainty baby basket can be made from cane, using a plywood base or a commercially-made basket can be bought made of wicker or rushes. The basket should be lined and although a machine-quilted fabric could be used, the whole effect will be much more beautiful if the material is decoratively quilted with fine hand stitchery. The lining should preferably be of cotton such as poplin, lawn, sateen or any fabric which does not have a shiny surface.

A pattern of the basket sides and base should be made carefully so that the lining which is cut from them will be a good fit.

Making a pattern
1. *Base pattern:* Take a piece of brown paper and place it centrally in the bottom of the basket. Press the paper firmly down all round the inside of the base so that an impression of the shape of the base, at the bottom of the stakes is made on the paper. Trim the surplus paper from the pattern.
2. *Side pattern:* Take a long piece of paper and place this round the inside of one half of the basket. Press the paper firmly down along the base at the bottom of the stakes and up under the top edge, marking the shape with a pencil. Make tucks in the paper along the base where necessary to get a good fit. Trim the surplus paper from the pattern. Place this $\frac{1}{2}$ pattern along a fold of a larger piece of paper and cut out, so that when opened out it makes a complete pattern of the inside of the basket. Try this pattern against the inside of the basket and adjust or trim where necessary to get a perfect fit.

Materials
$\frac{3}{4}$ yard of fine cotton
$\frac{3}{4}$ yard of synthetic wadding
$\frac{3}{4}$ yard of butter muslin
matching thread

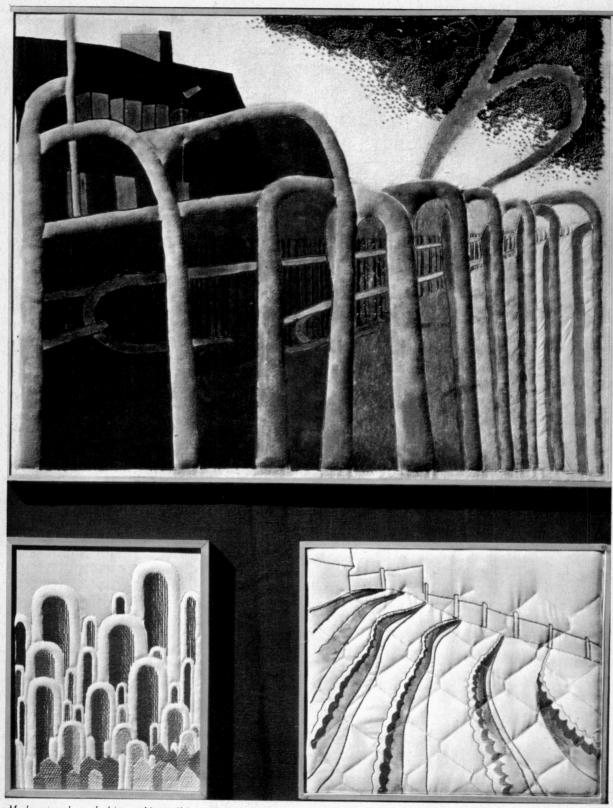

Modern panels worked in machine quilting techniques combined with embroidery.
(Sally Hayward, top and right ; Marion Gilling, left)

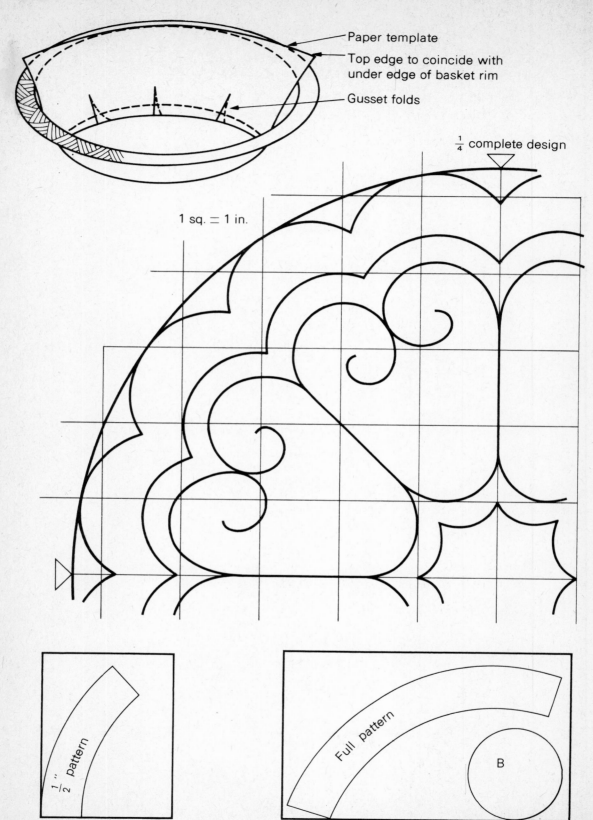

Paper template

Top edge to coincide with
under edge of basket rim

Gusset folds

¼ complete design

1 sq. = 1 in.

½ pattern

Full pattern

B

Fig 20

Method

Place both pieces of pattern on the wadding and muslin in turn and cut out. Pin the paper patterns on the lining fabric as shown in the diagrams and outline the seam allowances on the material with running stitches in coloured cotton. Remove the patterns. Put the fabric face down on a flat surface and place the wadding and then the muslin inside the coloured outlines, basting them carefully in position for quilting. The quilting process can be carried out by mounting on a frame or the stitchery can be worked in the hand. Choose a simple design which will be suitable for the area to be quilted or make a template from the illustration and work in the wadded quilting technique lining the basket.

When the quilting stitchery has been completed the pieces should be cut out along the coloured outline. Sew the side seams together and trim.

Cut a cardboard shape from the base pattern making it $\frac{1}{4}$ inch smaller all round. Run a gathering thread round the outside of the quilted base and place the cardboard circle on the underside of the quilted fabric. Pull the material round the shape by tightening the gathering thread until it is firmly in position. The design should be in the centre of the base on the right side of the work.

Using a long thread, lace the material across the back of the base and secure. The lower edges of the quilted sides are now pinned and sewn in position round the base and any slight fullness carefully adjusted. Place the lining in the basket before sewing to check the fitting.

When the two pieces of quilting have been joined the lining can be inserted and the base held in position with spots of adhesive on the wooden base.

Turn in the seam allowance at the top edge of the lining and adjust snugly and smoothly before starting to sew it in position. Use a cotton thread which matches the basket colouring so that the stitches will not show. Stitch the lining in place with stitches which go round the stakes of the basket on the outside and are invisible on the inside. When the basket has no decorative edge a border of lace trimming can be added.

Decorative straps can be made to hold articles such as talcum powder and these can be fitted round the quilted lining. A small pin cushion can be made and quilted with a design to match the basket, and this can be suspended from the basket edge.

Beach Bag (*Illustrated in colour, Page 20*)

Usually a beach bag is needed for one season only and it should be smart and gay as well as being a useful accessory to a beach outfit. One can easily be made from a piece of furnishing fabric if it is the correct colour, and brightly printed with a bold design. With careful selection it is possible to find a suitable piece of fabric which will become even more interesting when it is quilted by hand or, much more quickly, with a sewing machine.

Materials

$\frac{1}{2}$ yard of furnishing fabric 48 in. wide
1 yard of synthetic wadding or batt
matching sewing thread
$\frac{1}{2}$ yard of sateen lining 48 in. wide
1 pair of bamboo ring handles

Method

Plan the area of material to be quilted so that any pattern can be joined

Modern panel showing the use of the Italian quilting technique. (Elizabeth Gault)

correctly on the side seam. Trim away any unwanted material.

Baste or tack the wadding to the wrong side of the fabric with several rows of stitchery in both directions so that the two fabrics lie flat and are firmly held in place.

Consider the fabric design carefully and choose a suitable motif which can be picked out for quilting. Should the pattern be unsuitable, the surface of the material can be quilted all over with straight lines forming diamonds or squares.

Making-up
When the machine quilting has been completed the ends of the cut threads should be taken to the back of the work and fastened off and the basting cottons removed. Join the bottom edges of the bag and sew the side seams together for 9 inches from the lower edge. Leave the upper-side open and make a corresponding opening on the other side of the bag by cutting through the quilted fabric.

Dart the quilting at the top of the bag so that the fabric is tapered to fit the circular handles. Cut away any surplus material. Press open all the seams so that they lie flat.

Turn down the material at the open edges of the bag on both sides and stitch neatly with small herring bone stitches. Pin the bag handles in place and sew the fabric carefully and firmly in position so that both rings are level.

Cut and make a lining to fit the bag and pin it in position so that it lies flat inside the bag. Fit and pin the lining along the side openings and slip stitch the lining in place. Turn in the top edge of the lining under the handles, pleating the fabric neatly to make a good fit and slip stitch the fabric in place.

A Water Bottle Cover (*Illustrated in colour, Page 20*)
This small practical piece of work can be made quickly as it is quite simple and can be quilted easily. Made from a remnant of velvet it can be a most acceptable gift which will, in fact, cost surprisingly little to make as the pieces of fabric required are quite small.

Try to find a piece of left-over velvet large enough to make the two sides and some crossway strips for the cover, enough material matching or contrasting for the lining, a piece of old blanket or flannel as an inter-lining and a piece of fine net curtaining or muslin for the backing.

The overall size of the pieces required for each side is 16 inches by 12 inches.

Materials
2 pieces of velvet for the cover and a 2 yard length of
   crossway strip 1 in. wide
1 spool of matching thread
2 pieces of flannel
2 pieces of muslin or net for backing
2 pieces of silk for lining
2 yards of narrow piping cord
6 in. of Velcro

Method
Design details for the water bottle cover are shown, Fig. 21. Draw the outline shape or making-up line, the cutting line and the quilting design on a piece of paper, enlarged from the diagram, and check the

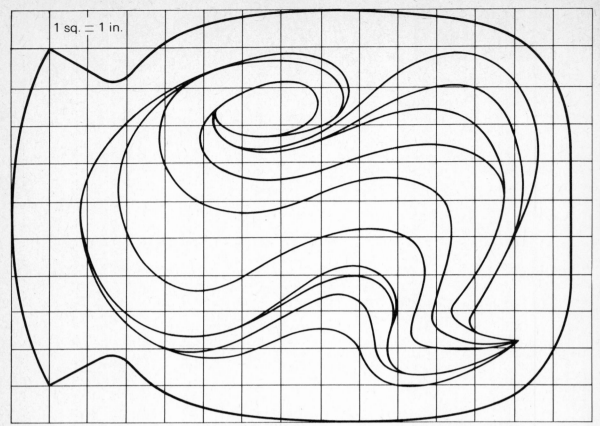

1 sq. = 1 in.

Fig 21

outline for accuracy with the actual water bottle. Pin the muslin or net over the design and trace off the cutting line, making up line and design using a fine fibre-tipped pen. Repeat on the muslin or net backing for the second side.

Steam velvet if required, to remove any marks, and with a warm iron smooth away any creases in the lining fabric. The velvet pile should run from top to bottom of the case and ensure that both pieces are correctly placed before putting them face down on a flat surface. Put the interlining smoothly on top with the transferred backing in position on the interlining. Secure at the edges with pins. Baste the three layers of fabric together with two or three rows of stitchery from top to bottom and from right to left, as well as making a row of stitches round the outer edges to prevent any puckering.

Quilting process
The quilting is worked in running stitches using the silk thread, and the stitches should be evenly spaced. Work until all the outlines of the design have been completed. The quilting can be carried out in the hand, and not mounted in a frame. Repeat for the second side.

Making-up
The pieces of quilting should be trimmed to the cutting line and the interlining and backing attached closely along the making-up line to the underside of each by basting. The surplus is trimmed off beyond the line of stitching.

Prepare the cord in the crossway strip and stitch it in place all round the making up line of one of the quilted pieces, so that it is in a continuous line. Join the cord and the ends of the crossway binding so that they are smooth and neat.

On the second quilted side use the remaining covered piping cord to outline the bottom opening of water bottle cover. This should neatly taper away at both ends on the sides, where it will merge with the front of the cover.

Slip stitch the back of the cover to the front along the base of the piping cord, starting and finishing securely on the sides of the opening.

Cut and stitch the lining to match the bottle cover but making it $\frac{1}{8}$ inch smaller all round. Fit the lining inside the work and trim if necessary. Sew the lining in place along the open edge up to the base of the piping. Fit a strip of "Velcro" on both sides of the opening on the inside to make a closure.

Remove any basting cottons from the work and carefully steam the velvet surface to raise the pile.

Cotton Hand Bag (*Illustrated in colour, Page 20*)

This small hand bag can be made from a piece of fabric left over from a cotton dress. The surface of the fabric is quilted, using a machine or worked by hand, and this process will give the fabric firmness as well as adding decoration. A zip fastener can be fitted to a pocket which can be inserted on the outer cover or fitted inside the bag along the edge of the lining seam.

Materials
1 piece of cotton measuring 18 in. by 30 in.
$\frac{1}{3}$ yard of lining to match 36 in. wide
1 spool of matching thread
$\frac{1}{2}$ yard of stiff muslin or Vylene
$\frac{1}{2}$ yard of cotton wadding or batt
1 zip fastener 8 in. long
2 pieces of bias binding, 18 in.
2 pieces of thin dowel rod 6$\frac{1}{2}$ in. long

Method
Enlarge the four pattern pieces from figure 22 on a sheet of brown paper and cut out the pattern shapes.

Place muslin wadding and cotton together and pin the three layers flat. Put the pattern for the bag cover on one half of the cotton fabric, so that it is central and square to any printed design. Outline the complete shape with close basting stitches and baste another line $\frac{1}{4}$ inch inside. These are the cutting and making-up lines.

Pin the pattern on the other half of the fabric and outline the cutting area making-up lines to correspond.

With a ruler as a straight-edge, mark with a row of pins the first two lines of quilting and stitch along these lines with a contrasting basting thread. These are the guide lines of the quilting.

Quilting process
Set up the machine with the quilting attachment and test the tension of the spare material along the edge of the work to ensure that it is correct. Set the quilting gauge so that the lines will be spaced 1$\frac{1}{2}$ inches apart. Commence the machine quilting, using the basted lines as guides, and quilt the fabrics in both directions for both sides of the bag.

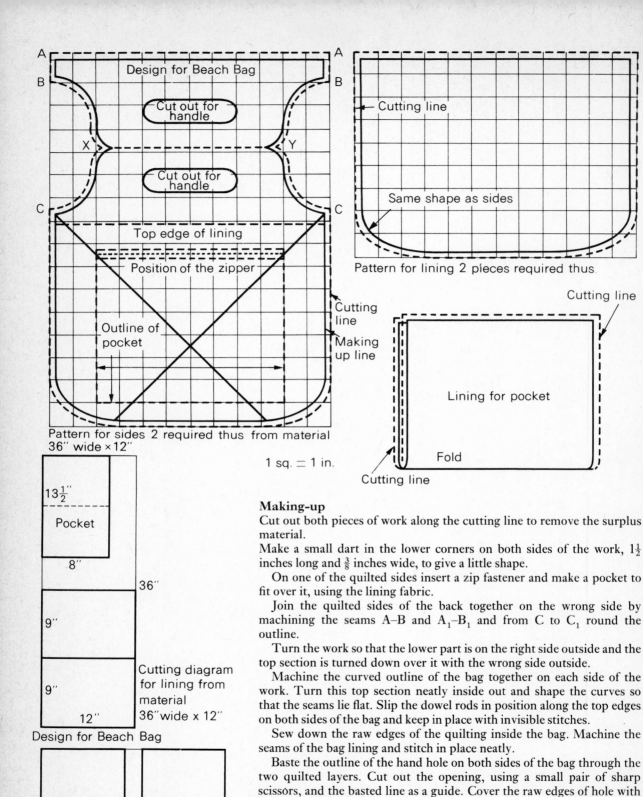

A

B

Design for Beach Bag

Cut out for handle

X

Y

Cut out for handle

C

Top edge of lining

Position of the zipper

Outline of pocket

Pattern for sides 2 required thus from material 36" wide ×12"

1 sq. = 1 in.

A

B

Cutting line

C

Same shape as sides

Pattern for lining 2 pieces required thus

Cutting line

Making up line

Cutting line

Lining for pocket

Fold

Cutting line

$13\frac{1}{2}$"

Pocket

8"

36"

9"

9"

12"

Cutting diagram for lining from material 36" wide x 12"

Design for Beach Bag

Cutting diagram for fronts from material 36" wide ×12"

Fig 22

Making-up

Cut out both pieces of work along the cutting line to remove the surplus material.

Make a small dart in the lower corners on both sides of the work, $1\frac{1}{2}$ inches long and $\frac{3}{8}$ inches wide, to give a little shape.

On one of the quilted sides insert a zip fastener and make a pocket to fit over it, using the lining fabric.

Join the quilted sides of the back together on the wrong side by machining the seams A–B and A_1–B_1 and from C to C_1 round the outline.

Turn the work so that the lower part is on the right side outside and the top section is turned down over it with the wrong side outside.

Machine the curved outline of the bag together on each side of the work. Turn this top section neatly inside out and shape the curves so that the seams lie flat. Slip the dowel rods in position along the top edges on both sides of the bag and keep in place with invisible stitches.

Sew down the raw edges of the quilting inside the bag. Machine the seams of the bag lining and stitch in place neatly.

Baste the outline of the hand hole on both sides of the bag through the two quilted layers. Cut out the opening, using a small pair of sharp scissors, and the basted line as a guide. Cover the raw edges of hole with a narrow bias binding.

Make a small piece of bias binding into a flat band and fit this through the end of the zip fastener as a decoration.

Bed quilts

A quilt consists of three different types of material. First the top layer of chosen fabric and a matching, toning or contrasting piece of fabric for the underside. The third layer consists of a padding between the other two. All three layers are held together with stitchery which should be planned to follow an interesting design.

Country women in the past evolved simple and beautiful designs using household utensils as templates; cups, saucers, plates, and glasses made different-sized circles, while the shapes of flowers, leaves, feathers and shells made their work lively and imaginative.

The shapes or templates which other quilters used were cut out of card, stiff paper, tin or plywood, and each quilter had a collection. Many would have been handed down from one generation to another.

The templates gave the outline of the shape and the filling in of the remainder.

Planning a quilt

When a large quilt is being made it will probably be necessary to use more than one width of fabric. It should never be made by piecing the fabric down the centre of the quilt. The full width should run down the centre and any additional material which is needed should be equally divided and joined on either side. It is preferable to first cut off the selvedges which could show through the quilt. Many quilters join the seams on the top of the quilt by hand and machine those on the underside. These will get more wear and stitching by machine will be stronger and much more satisfactory.

Where seams are made on a quilt top, it is sometimes possible to incorporate these joins into the actual design so that they do not show. Alternatively the added pieces of material could be a different colour or design, thus emphasising the piecing. Often the design can be freehand. New shapes often have to be made so that the design is in scale with the overall size of the work.

Making templates

Simple templates can be made by drawing on card and cutting out the shapes. Some can be made by folding paper and cutting out a simple shape.

Borders

These can be made by folding a long strip of paper in a concertina fold of four, six or more sections. Cut a shape out of the top and bottom and be careful to leave one place on either side of the paper, where the sections are attached. Open out, inspect and refold to make additional cuts if necessary. This method of making a design is very useful and becomes considerably easier with practise.

Centre Motif

To make a central motif take a piece of squared paper of the required size and fold it in four or eight. Cut a simple shape from the outside edges and from the centre, being careful to leave a place along the folded sides where the paper is attached. Open out, inspect and refold to make further cuts and modifications to the shape.

When a suitable design has been made, the paper shape can be pasted on a sheet of card which is cut to the outline on the paper and then used as a template.

Baby Cot Quilt

(32 in. by 22 in.)

The gift of a quilt for a new baby would be a perfect present. It could be made of finely woven pure silk, with a matt surface. Pink or blue on the top and white on the under side. Wool could be used for an interlining which is an ideal filling for lightness and warmth.

The quilt design is based entirely on traditional motifs and the quilting has been worked simply with no part of the design having double lines. The background fillings are well chosen, the small square diamond filling inside the feather motifs contrasting well with the bolder shapes of the feathers. Large square diamonds are used to fill the small remaining area in the centre of the quilt. The quilt design will be seen to have one main shape, made into a larger motif and used to fill each of the corners. This design has been extended in length to fill the remaining space along the two sides. A secondary shape has been made to fit the triangular space between the feathers, in the centre and at the top and bottom of the quilt. One background pattern only has been chosen to harmonise with the main scheme yet contrasting with its curving shapes.

The general impression of the quilt is one of softness and lightness, due mainly to the fact that the design unit is a simple and interesting shape which exactly fits the space available. When making a design for a small quilt, use fewer motifs than for a full-sized one and never try to reduce the pattern from a large quilt. Design with shapes made on a smaller scale, which are in proportion to the quilts overall dimensions. Aim at simplicity and although this can be achieved by using more straight lines and fewer curved, it is possible that by over simplification the design may lose something and become less lively and effective.

Materials

$\frac{3}{4}$ yard of pastel coloured crêpe de chine
1 yard of white crêpe de chine
3 spools of white pure silk thread
1 between needle No.9
1 small quilt frame
Padding for a quilt 32 in. by 22 in.
$3\frac{1}{4}$ yds of medium-size piping cord

Preparation of materials

Press the silk fabrics with a warm iron to remove any creases and shrink the piping cord by boiling it in hot water for a few minutes. Cut each of the pieces of fabric to measure 33 inches by 23 inches and prepare enough crossway binding 1 inch wide from the remainder of the white silk to go round the edge of the completed quilt.

Prepare the frame and set up the bottom cover in the centre of the webbing. If wool is being used as an interlining, it should be carefully

10″   centre

$14\frac{1}{2}$

Baby cot quilt $\frac{1}{4}$ complete design

prepared as described and, after being carded, should be laid gently on the fabric of the bottom cover, a little at a time so that the staple lies in one direction. It should go up to the edges of the work and be placed over the fabric in an even layer with no gaps.

Cotton wadding should be warmed first to make it fluffy and if this is used it should be handled carefully so that the layer is an even thickness.

The top cover is laid on and should fit perfectly. It can be already completely needle-marked or have only part of the design marked on the quilt top, the remainder to be added as the work progresses.

The top cover is firmly basted to the edge or near side of the frame through all three layers. Taking care to ensure that the fabrics are smooth, pin the cover in position on the opposite edge.

A length of tape is now attached to the stretchers and needled to the sides of the work using needles or fine steel pins to hold the three fabrics at intervals of 3 inches down the sides of the frame. This will hold the fabrics firmly but not tightly in position. The design could be needle-marked at this stage if preferred.

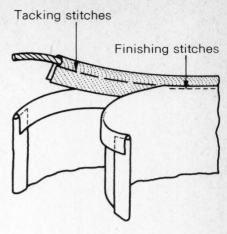

Tacking stitches

Finishing stitches

Method

Thread the needle with the silk thread and make a knot in the thread. Bring the needle up from under the work and give a small tug so that the knot will come through the outer fabric but not through the top. Make two or three running stitches at a time and hold the fore and middle finger of the left hand under the frame, pressing against the fabric the fore finger, feeling the needle tip each time it goes through the three layers. When the thread has been used up, take one stitch back over the last stitch or two, running the end away through the padding and bringing the needle up some distance away so that the thread can be cut off.

Making-up

When all the stitchery has been completed the work can be removed from the frame and enough crossway strips cut from the left-over fabric to cover the length of piping cord. (Fig. 23, top)

The corners of the quilt can be marked with a coin and trimmed so that they are rounder, to simplify the filling of the cord at the corners of the work. Stitch the cord in position on the front of the quilt and join cord and crossway strip neatly and invisibly. The cord should be attached with small running stitches on the surface to match the quilt. On the underside of the quilt the edges of the fabric are turned up to the base of the piping and attached with a row of running stitches through the layers of fabric but not going completely through to the other side.

When all the hand work has been completed, the quilt should be hung in a warm place to make the padding fluff up, which will add considerably to its appearance.

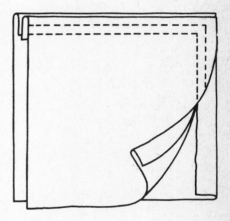

Quilt edgings

Junior Quilt (*Illustration in colour, Page 53*)

A practical and rather charming quilt can be made with applied motifs, made either from patchwork or cut from a remnant of printed fabric. Nursery scenes, animals, toys, or soldiers can be chosen to decorate the quilt top and these can be applied to the surface of the quilt in several ways.

1. The edges of the design can be turned under and sewn down invisibly with blind hemming stitches.
2. The edges can be sewn down with decorative surface stitchery. The design is tacked in position and the raw edges of the motif can be

covered with small close stitchery such as buttonhole stitch. This can be carried out in one colour only, or the colour of the embroidery thread can be changed so that it matches the outline of the design and merges into it. 3. The designs can be machined to the background fabric and the raw edges covered with close machine stitches.

Machine stitchery is used to apply the designs to the Junior Quilt, and a remnant of printed cotton printed with animal shapes is used for the appliqué design. The first step in the construction of this quilt is to cut out the designs from the remnant of material leaving $\frac{3}{4}$ inch of fabric round the edge of each motif.

Designs made from patchwork should first be drawn to scale on paper and then cut into simple templates which can be used for sewing the fabric together in the patchwork technique. Brightly-coloured scraps of material can be used for these designs which can be made up of plain or printed fabric. It is important that the pieces should be of the same type and thickness, preferably of cotton.

Materials
(*for a quilt size 30 in. by 54 in.*)
3 yards of firm cotton fabric
1 piece of synthetic wadding or batt 36 in. by 54 in.
5 yards of medium piping cord
Sewing thread to match the fabric
A collection of decorative motifs

Method
Cut the fabric as shown in the diagram and place the piece for the quilt top on a flat surface. Using a contrasting thread, baste a line of long running stitches about $4\frac{1}{2}$ inches from the edge of the material. Place the decorative shapes inside the stitched area and arrange them in an interesting position.

Baste them in position on the quilt top. If the designs are to be applied by machine it is important to remember to place a sheet of typing paper under the two thicknesses of material. If this is pinned in position and basted to the back of the quilt top, under the design, it will prevent any puckering or bunching. The paper can be torn away when the machining has been completed.

Test the machine stitching and tension on similar odd pieces of fabric to ensure that these are correct before commencing work. Use the zig-zag foot and machine round the edges of all the shapes along their outlines, using small, close stitching. Trim away the surplus material very carefully from the edge of all the designs, replace the foot with the satin stitch attachment, and cover the zig zag edges with close satin stitches. The designs are now neatly and firmly attached to the background fabric. Remove basting cottons, and fasten off.

Small designs can be padded by running thick wool into the back of the fabric, using a rug needle, while larger shapes can be padded with pieces of surplus wadding left over from the quilt pad. This should be done by first making a slit in the centre of the appliqué shape on the back of the quilt, being careful not to cut the surface fabric. Push pieces of loose wadding through the hole with a stuffing needle. This should be evenly and smoothly spread all over the appliqué shape and if necessary worked into any corners with a bodkin. Do not over stuff the designs or the fabric around the shapes will pucker. When enough stuffing has been inserted the slit is closed with a neat whip stitch.

Fig 24

Making-up

From the left over fabric, cut and join a sufficient amount of $1\frac{1}{4}$ inch wide bias strips to cover the piping cord. Baste the piping cord in position inside the bias binding. Place the top and bottom quilt covers together right sides facing. Insert the covered piping cord and pin it between the two edges of the material and tack it in position. Ease the cord at each corner and cut three 'V' shaped notches from the bias strip to allow it to lie flat and neatly in position when it is turned inside out. The crossway strip and piping should be joined as inconspicuously as possible. At the bottom of the quilt, leave an opening so that the filling can be inserted. Machine the quilt along the piping, using a piping foot or stitching with the ordinary foot sitting on top of the piping cord all the time to ensure close stitchery. Trim the fabric at the corners to make less bulk and turn the quilt cover to right side. Insert the piece of sheet wadding or batt and trim if necessary to ensure that it is a good fit. Slip stitch the edges of the opening together invisibly, and quilt the three thicknesses of material together along the coloured basting line, removing the thread when the work is complete.

The three layers could be held together with neat tie tacks in several places on the underside of the quilt. These will hold the materials firmly in place, though the tie tacks can be cut carefully and the slip stitched opening undone so that the filler can be removed to allow the cotton cover to be washed when necessary.

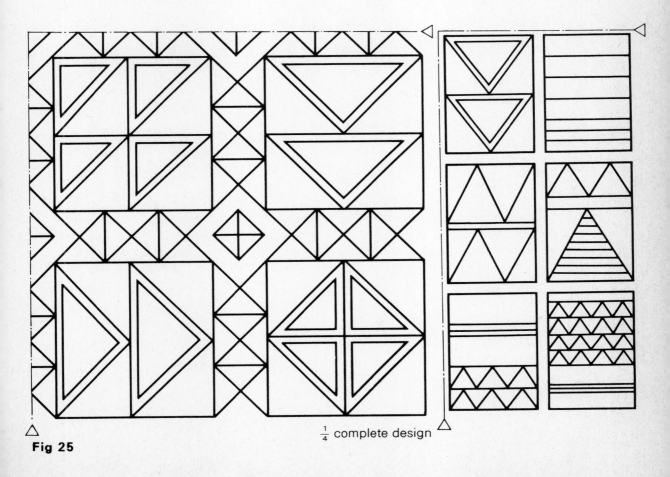

$\frac{1}{4}$ complete design

Fig 25

73

Single Quilt *(Illustrated in colour, Page 56)*

Tomorrow's Heirloom

This beautiful quilt has been developed from a design based on straight lines and triangles which together form a very interesting scheme. The design has been worked in wadded quilting but it could be interpreted equally well in the corded quilting technique (Fig. 25).

The fabric chosen for the top cover is a deep orange with a matching cotton for the underside. A synthetic batting or wadding has been used as an underlay. This is very resilient material and its thickness makes the quilted design stand out in high relief.

The quilt measures 94 inches by 71 inches overall and it has an 18 inch border around the quilted design. The quilted area measures 67 inches by 42 inches. This should be worked first and the side borders added in the making up process. A frame is an absolute necessity and all quilts should be worked on a substantially made quilting frame with strong members which will not warp or bend.

Materials

Top Cover – $5\frac{1}{4}$ yards Clydella 36 in. wide
Bottom Cover – $5\frac{1}{4}$ yards of Cotton 36 in. wide
Thread – 2 spools of mercerised cotton No.40
Underlay – 2 yards of synthetic batting or wadding $\frac{1}{2}$ in.
thick 42 ins. wide

Method

The fabrics for the top and bottom cover should be cut in half and one piece of each put aside for the borders.

The Clydella and cotton should be marked to show the position of the quilted area, i.e. $9\frac{3}{4}$ inches from the top edge and $16\frac{3}{4}$ inches from the bottom of the quilt. The top cover should be chalk or needle marked with the full design or with part of it.

Stitch the bottom cover of the quilt to the webbing along the top and bottom rollers of the frame so that it is centrally placed on both bars. Place the top cover over the bottom cover so that the marks of the quilted area correspond, and attach the fabric along the near edge roller of the frame. Roll the near end fabrics evenly round the bar, up to the design area, and ensure that there are no creases.

Pin back the surplus fabric of the top cover and roll the fabric of the bottom cover round the far roller, holding the fabric taut by stretching the rollers apart and fixing pegs in the holes.

Place the padding in position on the bottom cover, up to the edges of the design area, and up in the marked top cover so that it lies smooth and flat over the two fabrics. Pin firmly along the top of the far edge of the frame. Hold the sides of the fabric with tape needled to the three layers of material and laced round the stretchers.

There will be wadding and the fabric of the top cover hanging over the far edge of the frame. This should be rolled loosely and fastened to the top of the work so that it will not fall on the floor.

The quilting should be worked as neatly as possible with even running stitches and very straight lines and as the work progresses the finished quilting should be rolled on to the near bar and the unquilted fabrics released from the other end. This should always be done as carefully as possible to ensure that the quilting is not creased.

When the quilting has been completed and taken off the frame it should be hung in a warm place, for some time. The fabrics for the border should be cut in half and one piece of each should be stitched down the quilt on each side of the quilt top so that the fabrics match.

The edges of both fabrics should be turned in all round the outer edge of the quilt and stitched flat with one row of neat running stitches.

Design for a Double Quilt

The design is for a quilt 4 feet square and could be used for wadded or corded quilting. The quilted area should be surrounded by at least 18 inches of plain area to cover the bed to floor level. Alternatively use a border design on the surround, using some of the quilt motifs.

Traditional Quilt Designs

Small Quilt (*Illustrated in colour, Page 24*)
(*Size 41 ins. by 27 ins.*)

This charming piece of work is based on the Durham feather pattern which, in the centre of the design, is made to encircle a rose. Around the edge of the quilt a border of traditional running feather has been carefully planned to follow the corners and central design. Square diamond pattern has been used for the background and makes a perfect contrast to the flowing curves of the traditional shapes.

The quilting has been worked on pure silk, a deep orange for the top of the quilt and lemon on the underside. The stitchery has been worked with orange silk thread, matching the darker colour of the two fabrics. The edge has been turned in with two rows of running stitches ¾ inch apart.

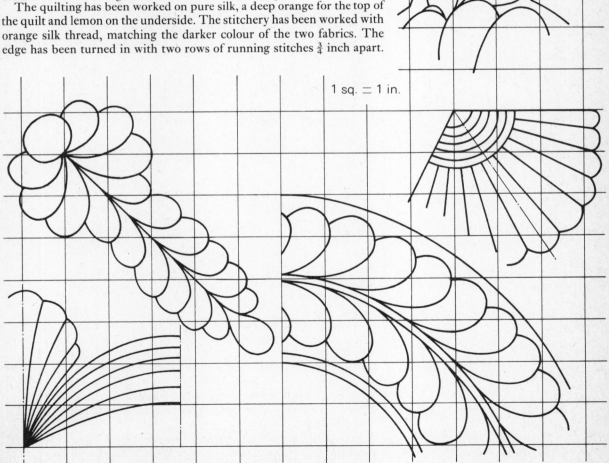

1 sq. = 1 in.

Fig 26

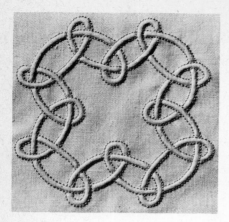

Single Bed Quilt (*Illustrated in colour*, Page 24)

(*Size 40 ins. by 70 ins.*) (See also Fig. 26)

Many traditional shapes have been used in the design of this lovely Durham quilt. The beautiful designed oval which forms the centre motif has been made up of four goosewing templates and two fans. These are enclosed by a continuous running feather. A finely worked border has been carefully planned with a cord and tassel design.

The quilt top has been decorated with rose feather and fan templates, and their shapes stand out against a background of square diamonds.

Pure silk has been used for both sides of the quilt, in a deep shade of blue. The edge of the quilt has been finished with a very fine piping cord encased in a bias binding.

A thin layer of wool has been used for the interlining and the three layers have been stitched together with even running stitches so that the work is completely reversible and perfect on both sides.

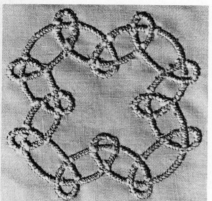

Wadded Quilt (*Illustrated in colour*, Page 52)

In this old wadded quilt the top cover is of natural-coloured sateen and the bottom cover of cream sateen, patterned with a small design of deep pink floral shapes. It is a very small print which unfortunately obscures the quilted stitchery, which can really only be seen at all clearly on the quilt top.

Four traditional designs have been used on the quilt, which has a large rose in the centre, rows of wide cable bee shapes in the corners, and two beautiful bands of running feather on either side of the central motif. The quilt which measures $81\frac{1}{2}$ inches wide and $85\frac{1}{2}$ inches long was probably made in Durham at the end of the last century. It is not a masterpiece but a simple piece of work and one which has a great deal of charm.

Linen Quilting

Linen quilting can be used in a way that is not only decorative and useful but to add an extremely personal touch to clothes, table linen or to gifts.

The technique of linen quilting can be used on table or bed linen to decorate it or to identify the article permanently. An initial can be designed which is framed with corded quilting and this can be worked on to bed linen and table napkins making a charming addition to rather plain items.

When a monogram or decoration is added to table napkins or handkerchiefs it should always be worked with the base of the shape facing the corner.

Linen Quilting

Corded technique

Fig 27

Linen Quilted Cover

This beautiful sample of Georgian quilting was probably made in the early eighteenth century and at that time formed part of the furnishing of a bed.

The top cover is made of very finely woven linen with closely woven linen scrim on the underside. The stitching of the decorative motifs has been worked in minute back stitches and the curving lines of the background worked in fine running stitches so that the two layers of material are joined closely.

Every small channel and minute section of the design has been padded with strands of unravelled cord threaded through the back of the work so that the design stands out in relief.

Thrift Quilt (*Illustrated in colour*, *Page 57*)

Quilting has always been a thrifty craft making use of worn materials or scraps of fabric from the piece bag. Early patchwork evolved from the economic use of beautiful scraps of material left over from dressmaking, which were too costly to discard. Good pieces of worn garments were frequently used by our forebears for simple coverlets and quilts in a thrifty and not necessarily decorative way.

This is illustrated in the simple version of the log cabin design used on a thrift quilt made by a very old lady many years ago. All the strips in this quilt are good pieces from old garments such as shirts, apron blouses and cotton dresses. The quilt has a particular charm in spite of its obvious simplicity and it was made for thrifty rather than aesthetic reasons.

Patchwork Quilt (*Illustrated in colour*, *Page 61*)

The patchwork of this quilt was also made many years ago and again illustrates the thrifty use of fabric scraps. Here travellers' samples were made into hexagons, joined in rosettes, and stitched to a background of plain cotton shapes. The main piece of patchwork has been mounted on a quilt top with a number of rosettes applied round the edge.

Interlining

Old thin blankets were frequently used as an interlining for many quilts, often as an economic necessity. The three layers of the quilt can be held together with quilting, but sometimes a quicker method can be adopted. The layers can be held together with tie knots, which are described in the next paragraph.

Tie Knots

The interlining should not be cotton wadding as it will not be held in position closely enough over the quilt. It should be sheet wadding or dacron batt, old blanket or flannel sheet. When the work is ready for padding, the quilt backing should be spread on the floor, face down. The filling should be spread over the backing and this should be covered with the quilt top, placed in position right side up. Work from the centre, pinning and basting all three layers carefully making sure that they are flat.

Tie knots can be made at regular intervals over the quilt, hidden in the surface decoration or pattern. They should be made so that no large areas are left untied.

The knots are made using a long sharp needle threaded with a strand of thick embroidery silk. Pierce the surface of the quilt, going through the three layers at the chosen point, leaving about two inches of thread and coming back through the quilt surface about $\frac{1}{4}$ inch away. Cut the thread and tie the two ends in a reef knot as shown in the diagram and continue working across the quilt until all the knots are made. Trim each knot so that the ends are $\frac{1}{2}$ inch to 1 inch long as preferred.

Sheeps Wool Quilts

In districts where there are many sheep, it is possible to find wool which has been caught in the hedgerows or on barbed wire fences. This wool can be gathered at regular intervals and when enough has been found it can be used to fill small quilts.

Wool is probably the best filling for a quilt because of its lightness and warmth. It has however the tendency to become matted and lumpy unless handled correctly. It can be used very successfully to make a very simple type of thrift quilt made from a series of small bags. When the wool is collected it should be thoroughly washed several times in very hot soapy water until it is completely free from all grease and any dirt. It should then be rinsed in warm water, until the water is clean and free from soap. The wool should be squeezed and put to dry in a warm place. It will dry much more quickly if the fibres are pulled out well or teased with the fingers. This teasing should be done at frequent intervals until the wool is dry and as light as a feather. Make quite sure it is free from any lumps or small matted pieces.

The success of any quilt using wool will depend on this teasing and, should a large amount be washed and prepared, it is probably much easier to use a pair of hand carders, which will comb and straighten the wool staples until they are wispy light. This wool can be used most effectively for wadded quilts and is ideal for cot covers.

Wool with short wiry fibres is better than that with long fine ones, but all can be put to a very practical use and made into a warm coverlet or cot quilt using scraps of material left over from cotton dresses or from factory off cuts.

However the same method can be used with a synthetic filling specially prepared for the purpose.

Thrift Quilt Bag Method

(Size 30 inches × 20 inches)

This quilt is made from 25 bags measuring 6 inches by 4 inches. The method is suitable for a small quilt and its construction should be accurate to ensure that the elements fit together properly. All the pieces of material for the cover should be of a similar type and must not be transparent. Do not use any heavy fabric such as a furnishing material.

Preparation

Cut a piece of cardboard to the size you want for use as a template to ensure that all the pieces of fabric are of uniform size. Place the cardboard shape on the wrong side of the fabric along the grain in both directions.

Draw a line round the sides of the templates and cut out. Mark and cut the required number of pieces.

Making-up
Fold and sew each of the pieces of fabric in turn and make a bag measuring 6 inches by 4 inches in size.

Turn each bag inside out and fill with $\frac{1}{4}$ oz. of sheeps wool or synthetic filler; stitch the bag so that the top edge is closed. The bags can be sewn together in a number of ways, by slip stitching, blanket stitching or over-sewing.

A strong neat finishing can be made by slip stitching the bags together on both sides of the work. The same technique could be used with different shapes such as squares or hexagons, or random shapes combined to form a rectangular quilt shape.

Conclusion

In an age of mass production we are becoming more aware of the skills of the craftsmen and women who produce beautiful and individual work. The decoration of the home can be made entirely personal by the skilful addition of good craft work, and quilting is one of the ways in which the combination of colour and stitchery can be a perfect means of self expression. Many articles can be made using quilting techniques and the final result can be purely simple and practical or elaborately artistic. This craft gives great scope for the development of individual ideas in design and colour, enabling the beginner to produce interesting personal items and the more experienced worker to continue to experiment and develop the technique.

Glossary of Terms

Appliqué or applied work – Pieces of material cut out and sewn on to a background fabric.

Background – The bottom layer of a quilt as a whole or the lawn or butter muslin used behind the padding.

Binding – The process used to cover the edges of the work, sewing and holding them together to make a decorative edge.

Coverlet – A quilt which covers only the top of the bed without covering the pillows or hanging down the sides of the bed.

Corded quilting – The technique of sewing a cord to the underside of a design to raise it in relief on the surface of the fabric.

Dressing the frame – Mounting the fabrics in the frame for the quilting process.

English padding or linen quilting – A process used to pad only small areas of a design, unravelled cord or wool being used to stuff the shapes.

Padding – The middle layer of filling or underlay placed between the top and bottom covers of a quilt. It can be wool, cotton wool or one of the new synthetics such as terylene or dacron. It is also called batt wadding or stuffing.

Template – A shape or pattern cut from a durable material such as cardboard to outline the design on to the top fabric.

Top and bottom covers – The fabric of the two sides of a quilt.

Wadded quilting – The technique worked when three layers of material are sewn together with decorative stitchery.